Richard Harding Davis

The Great War Reporter

Journalism 1914-1916

The Archive of American Journalism

Lincoln Steffens

Henry Stanley

Theodore Roosevelt

Richard Harding Davis

Ida Tarbell

Ray Stannard Baker

Nellie Bly

H.L. Mencken

Ambrose Bierce

Stephen Crane

Jack London

Mark Twain

Ernest Hemingway

Richard Harding Davis

The Great War Reporter

Journalism 1914 - 1916

The Archive of American Journalism
St. Paul, Minnesota
2016

Note on Sources

All articles are complete and unabridged, with headlines, subheads and formatting that match the original publication. Minor edits have been made to correct obsolete spelling and punctuation. These are "public domain" texts that can be freely copied, reproduced and distributed without permission or cost. Please credit The Archive of American Journalism as your source.

We welcome your comments, suggestions, and ideas. Please contact us via e-mail at thegrandarchive@gmail.com or via US mail at the following address.

The Archive LLC
9269 Troon Court
Woodbury, MN 55125.

Our collection of the articles of Richard Harding Davis and 12 other American authors is now available at:
http:\\www.historicjournalism.com

Article selection and original Introduction copyright ©2016 by Tom Streissguth

**Library of Congress Control Number: 2015947322
ISBN: 978-0-9907137-4-6**

Acknowledgments

For their encouragement and suggestions, sincere thanks to Mark Lerner, Gordon Hagert, Pier Gustafson, Phil Gapp, Jonathan Peacock, John Hatch, Marian Streissguth and our original founding supporters: William F. Zeman, Phil Gapp, Walter Crowley, Adele Streissguth, Richard Prosser, Abhilash Sarhadi, and James McGrath Morris.

Table of Contents

Introduction
xi

The Lusitania, Taking Sporting Chance, Wins
New York Tribune/August 13, 1914
3

London, Though Eager for News, Gladly Yields to the Censor
New York Tribune/August 15, 1914
5

Davis Sure Germans Were Withdrawing
New York Tribune/August 20, 1914
6

Like a River of Steel It Flowed, Gray and Ghostlike
New York Tribune/August 23, 1914
7

Germans Got Cold Cheer in Brussels
New York Tribune/August 25, 1914
10

Horrors of Louvain Told by Eyewitness; Circled Burning City
New York Tribune/August 31, 2014
12

Germans Censor Notes of Envoys
New York Tribune/September 1, 1914
18

Tells Experience as War Prisoner
New York Tribune/September 2, 1914
22

Eight American Writers Arrested
New York Tribune/September 4, 1914
26

Says Kaiser, Breaking Word, Tricked Czar
New York Tribune/September 4, 1914
35

Paris Standing Strain of War Complacently
New York Tribune/September 15, 1914
38

Public Opinion Ends Aero Visits
New York Tribune/September 15, 1914
42

Vivid Description of the Shelling of Rheims Cathedral
New York Tribune/September 22, 1914
44

Rheims Cathedral Not Used by Army
New York Tribune/September 26, 1914
53

Rheims a Wreck Around Cathedral
New York Tribune/September 29, 1914
57

French Capital Sees Its Oldtime Activity
New York Tribune/October 3, 1914
63

The Germans in Brussels
Scribner's/November, 1914
68

The Appalling Waste of the European War
New York Tribune/November 1, 1914
81

"Under Fire"--By Richard Harding Davis
New York Tribune/November 8, 1914
92

Uncle Sam's Diplomats in War Zone Do Him Honor
New York Tribune/November 15, 1914
103

War Correspondents' Fight for Place in the Sun
New York Tribune/November 22, 1914
114

Rheims During the Bombardment
Scribner's/January, 1915
124

Wengler's "Two Shots"
The New York Times/January 8, 1915
134

An Insult to War
The New York Times/July 11, 1915
136

Poincaré Thanks America for Help
The New York Times/November 6, 1915
138

"War as Usual" Motto of France
The New York Times/November 16, 1915
142

Allies in Serbia Fighting in the Clouds
The New York Times/December 9, 1915
148

Allies at Saloniki Preparing to Stay
The New York Times/December 11, 1915
150

Arras, The Unburied City
The New York Times/December 12, 1915
151

Americans Escape Safely from Gievgeli
The New York Times/December 13, 1915
155

Allies' Casualties in Retreat Given as 1,700
The New York Times/December 15, 1915
158

Luring Teutons On To Saloniki
The New York Times/December 31, 1915
160

Air Raiders Aimed At Allies' Warships
The New York Times/January 2, 1916
164

Allies' Grip on Food Keeps Greece Still
The New York Times/January 12, 1916
166

French Made Merry in Serbian Retreat
The New York Times/January 19, 1916
171

A Deserted Command
The New York Times/January 23, 1916
179

A Peep at the Famous St. Mihiel Salient
The New York Times/February 6, 1916
187

The War That Lurks in the Forest of the Vosges
The New York Times/February 13, 1916
193

Blinded in Battle, But Not Made Useless
The New York Times/February 27, 1916
197

Verdun's Traps and Mazes
The New York Times/March 5, 1916
208

President Poincaré Thanks America
New York Times/November 6, 1916
211

Further Reading
226

Online Collections
227

From The Archive
228

Introduction

Early in the morning of January 19, 1897, a detail of Spanish infantry marched Adolfo Rodriguez to the moonlit outskirts of Santa Clara, a nondescript village of central Cuba. With his hands bound, and a murmuring priest following close behind, Rodriguez passed under the gaze of a tall, strapping American journalist, who found much to admire in the way a 20-year-old insurgent, his adult life barely begun, could so nonchalantly smoke a last cigarette and calmly, quietly stroll to his impending execution.

The reading public back in the States wanted thrills, danger and pathos from the Cuban insurgency. Richard Harding Davis was now standing in the early dawn at Santa Clara, and over the last weeks riding and roaming all over the island, to meet their demands. Telegraphed that same day to New York, "The Death of Rodriguez" immediately ran on the front page of William Randolph Hearst's *New York Journal*, causing a sensation. This was a new and powerful kind of journalism that painted an eloquent word picture of one man's courage in the face of death. It would also make Davis' reputation as the bravest and most flamboyant newspaperman alive, and to Hearst a writer well worth the ridiculously extravagant salary of $3,000 a month, plus expenses.

Just a few weeks earlier, in December, 1896, the Cuban insurgency against Spanish rule was taking lives and promising news. Davis set out aboard Hearst's private yacht, the *Vamoose*, in the company of artist Frederic Remington. When the yacht—reputed to be the largest private vessel in New York harbor—was turned back by a storm, Davis and Remington returned to Florida, where they took passage aboard a public ferry. After his arrival on the island, Davis found no fighting and not much of interest. Nevertheless, despite Hearst's proclamation in the *Journal* that his star reporter had encountered a revolt in full strength, Davis gamely soldiered on—while Remington returned to the States—and wrote home that:

> *I am just not in it and I am torn between coming home and ... getting one story to justify me being here and that damn silly page of the Journal's. All Hearst wants is my name and I will give him that only if it will be signed to a different sort of a story from those they have been printing.*

Davis never shied from a challenge, either physical or literary. Then again, he started out with every advantage. Born in 1864 in Philadelphia, he was the son of Rebecca Harding Davis, an acclaimed novelist and journalist, and Lemuel Clark Davis, editor of the Philadelphia *Public Ledger*. He attended Lehigh University as well as Johns Hopkins, and was expelled from both for neglecting his studies. Davis broke into the newspaper business when Lemuel Davis got him hired at the Philadelphia *Record*, and then moved on to crime reporting at the New York *Evening Sun*.

For Davis, a reporter's life was closely bound up with a reporter's image; the one he created was a doer of good deeds, a fighter of crime and social ills, a writer who creates memorable characters, human drama, unforgettable stories. While on the city beat, he made a well-publicized citizen's arrest of a notorious con artist, and eyewitnessed the first execution by electrocution in 1890. His newspaper work was a small part of his literary efforts; he also brought out plays, poems and short stories, drawn from the city's gritty real life, and after his death forgotten.

As his name grew familiar with the avid newspaper audience, Davis became a roving adventurer with integrity and a strong sense of the theatrical. Yet he was neither an anti-trust crusader in the spirit of Ida Tarbell nor a civic-minded muckraker in the Lincoln Steffens mold. In the year after the death of Adolfo Rodriguez, the Spanish-American War gave him the opportunity, as a correspondent for the New York *Herald*, to dress in tropical fatigues and search out danger, pathos and thrills along the front lines of an exotic and not-too-distant island. It was in Cuba that Davis encountered Theodore Roosevelt, and where the writer brought the tough-fibered military amateur from the front lines to the front page, setting the media stage for Roosevelt's rise to the White House. And it was in Cuba that Davis tendered his resignation to William Randolph Hearst for Hearst's over-the-top sensationalism and constant deception in the service of his newspaper's circulation numbers.

By this time, journalism had passed the age of the adventurer. James Gordon Bennett may have financed dangerous African expeditions by the intrepid Henry Stanley, but Hearst and his rivals needed men who would follow telegraphed instructions, limit expenses, and act as letter writers—"correspondents"—who would simply get to their destination and explain what they were seeing,

Davis became the model. Passport in hand, and camping kit locked snugly in his steamer trunk, he reached the Boer War in South Africa and the inner sanctum of the Kremlin in Moscow. He witnessed the German occupation of Belgium during World War I, and the ruthless colonial exploitation by the king of Belgium in the Congo, which brought out a heartfelt outrage at injustice—the stock-in-trade of the contemporary daily reporter.

Scribner's, *Collier's*, and the mass-circulation New York dailies sent him to report the Russo-Japanese war, to witness political oppression in Central America, and describe the fighting in Greece, where Davis applied his cool eye and stagey descriptions to a meaningless, bloody corner of World War I, "The Great War":

> The Greek rifles crackled and flashed at the lines, but the men below came on quite steadily, picking their way over

the furrows and appearing utterly unconscious of the seven thousand rifles that were calling on them to halt. They were advancing directly toward a little sugar-loaf hill, on the top of which was a mountain battery perched like a tiara on a woman's head. It was throwing one shell after another in the very path of the men below, but the Turks still continued to pick their way across the field, without showing any regard for the mountain battery. It was worse than threatening; it seemed almost as though they meant to insult us . . . the steady advance of so many men, each plodding along by himself, with his head bowed and his gun on his shoulder, was aggravating.

By the time Davis wrote this passage, he was not only the nation's most famous newspaperman, he was a star, a familiar brand with a trendy clean-shaven face and a matchless instinct for the public's voyeuristic interest in the tragic details of great events, thankfully happening elsewhere. He was well compensated for the work: *Scribner's* paid $1,000 for his articles, and the Wheeler Syndicate offered Davis a generous retainer of $600 a week to get as close to the front as possible in Europe.

By the time of the Great War, he was traveling in high style. As diplomacy failed in Europe, and the cascading declarations of war hit the telegraph wires, he departed for Europe aboard the Cunard liner *Lusitania* on August 4, 1914. Davis had gallantly engaged the ship's royal suite in order to keep his wife Bessie, then five months pregnant, as comfortable as possible. After reaching London, and setting Bessie down in a good hotel, he headed for Belgium, intending to place himself squarely in the path of the German army's advance towards northern France.

Taking up spacious quarters at the Palace Hotel in Brussels, Davis scanned the dailies for dispatches from the front, then hired a car to bring him as close to the action as the driver dared. His cars raced hither and yon over the flat and nearly featureless countryside, seeking and often finding active battle zones, before he returned to the city in the evening for dinner in good company, a bath and a comfortable bed.

On the morning of August 19, as the massive columns of gray-uniformed German infantry wound further west, the panic began. The wealthy fled Brussels, bringing along their butlers and servants. On the next day, the German army marched into Brussels along the Boulevard Waterloo. The awesome spectacle fascinated onlookers, and inspired writing that compelled readers of the New York *Tribune* to see, in every detail, what Davis had seen:

> At the sight of the first few regiments of the enemy we were thrilled with interest. After they had passed three hours in one unbroken steel-gray column, we were bored. But when hour after hour passed and there was no halt, no breathing time, no open spaces in the ranks, the thing became uncanny, inhuman. You returned to watch it, fascinated. It held the mystery and menace of fog rolling toward you across the sea.

A strict blackout on telegraph transmission was in effect; the article was smuggled out in the coats of a young English boy, E.A. Dalton, who walked, crawled and furtively ran through the German lines to get the dispatch to the coast at Ostend, and from there to England. As always with Davis, the simple facts of the reporter's existence became a central part of the story, and the drama, yet none of his many dramas could match that of his near-execution as an Allied spy.

On August 23, Davis and Gerald Morgan, an American reporting for the London *Telegraph*, engaged a taxi to the Allied lines at Halle. The taxi was intercepted by a German detachment, and its occupants placed under arrest. Forced to accompany the German army back to Brussels, Davis made the fateful decision to leave his companions behind and head back towards the front lines. Finding himself in the village of Enghien at dusk, he decided to spend the night in town and, if the conditions permitted, follow the German army further towards, and perhaps into France.

After some difficulty about finding a room, Davis spent a few hours calmly watching the German army pass. His goal was to be curtly ordered back to Brussels by a German officer, thus lending a convincing and picturesque conclusion to the dispatch he would write. The suspicious itinerary, however, did not escape notice by several German officers, who took him into custody and began debating whether to shoot him immediately or at dawn the next day. The intrepid reporter had unwittingly fallen in with a flanking maneuver ordered by the Germans to surprise the English; the Germans naturally assumed his intention was to warn the English army several miles ahead. Unfortunately, although Davis carried an American passport, it had been issued in London; worse, he was wearing a British military uniform.

Davis had an answer, however: his hat carried the label of "Knox, New York" (later taken up by Knox Hats in their advertising campaign). Confined to a whitewashed cell, the reporter proposed that he be given a pass allowing him two days to walk the 50 miles back to Brussels. Taken to a chateau stuffed with high-ranking officers, Davis was given his pass and permission to start walking—at three in the morning. After an hour-long slog in the dark, he flagged down a ride from a German general, who agreeably took him all the way to the outskirts of Brussels.

For Richard Harding Davis, the Great War was like that: drama mixed with fear, high comedy and lucky happenstance with dread. His eloquent and colorful articles never overlooked the terrors of war, however, nor did he hesitate to call out all sides for their wastefulness, cowardice, and wanton cruelty. For the modern reader browsing them a century later, these stories offer fascinating insights into the war's tangled history and a distinctive voice in the difficult, dangerous craft of battlefield reporting.

The Great War Reporter

Journalism 1914 - 1916

"GERMAN SUNK," SUFFOLK FLASHES

SENT TO BULGARIA IS GIVEN BY CZAR

PRINCE WOUNDED BY SHELL AT BELGRADE

FRENCH ANNIHILATE GERMAN REGIMENTS

THE LUSITANIA, TAKING SPORTING CHANCE, WINS

BOSTON ADOPTS EXCHANGE RULING

BRITAIN TO END TRADE DEADLOCK

FRENCH FIGHTING WELL; GERMANS MASS TROOPS

LIKE TO POSTPONE RACE, SAYS LIPTON

Hospital Ship Speeds to Canadian Cruiser

GERMANS AVOID FIGHT, SAYS BELGIAN REPORT

THE TRIBUNE'S Comprehensive Atlas of the World and European War Map

New York Tribune
August 13, 1914

The Lusitania, Taking Sporting Chance, Wins

**Most Welcome of All England's Reservist Ships,
After Slow but Tense Crossing,
Gets Royal Greeting in Her Home Port of Liverpool**

Liverpool, Aug. 12.—The home run of the *Lusitania* to Liverpool ended last night in safety. Where other ships feared to start, or, having started, put back, she took a sporting chance and won. Of all the reservist vessels returning to the colors, she is one of the most welcome here. The original cost of this vessel was $7,000,000. On this voyage she carried much gold, 800 bags of mail, 200 passengers and a crew of 800. Among the passengers were Lieutenant Porte, the British aviator; Sheldon Leavitt Crosby, secretary of the American Embassy at Madrid; M. Menier, the millionaire French chocolate manufacturer; Captain Miller, of the English polo team; Guy Standing, the actor, and Laura Guerite.

The panic, reported by passengers on the German ship *Kronprinzessin Cecilie*, that put back to Bar Harbor was conspicuously absent on this ship. Discipline was strict, but all on board recognized that precaution was being taken against capture. To sailors and to passengers the ship's log was a closed book, but several incidents were witnessed by all.

The first day out a torpedo boat destroyer gave us a scare, but she was apparently American and, after looking us over, turned back. Later in the day we held up the *Pannonia*, and as we dared not use our wireless, we gave her good advice by semaphore signs. Since then no other ship was sighted.

Yesterday morning we signaled the station at Bull, Cow and Calf, and were curtly told to haul down our flag. The trip was very much like any other. The passengers indulged in bridge, deck games and listening to band concerts.

Lest it might establish our position, no wireless was sent, but many bulletins were snatched from the air. One, stating we had been captured by German cruisers, was by those on board generally discredited.

The *Lusitania*'s voyage was the slowest on her record, for the reason that one of her turbine engines broke down the second day out.

New York Tribune
August 15, 1914

London, Though Eager for News, Gladly Yields to the Censor

London, Aug. 14. — On arriving in London what most impresses you is, in the English papers, the absence of any news concerning any movement of the English navy and army. It is a conspiracy of silence on the part of the English people of the most unselfish and patriotic nature.

No interest at this time in any relative with any ship or regiment is permitted to outweigh the wishes of all for the success of all. This secrecy as to the present plans or whereabouts of any military unit is enforced not only by the orders of the War Office, but is the wish of every one.

A father, son or brother leaves to join his ship or regiment, and after that his family neither know nor seek to know where he may be. It is a splendid compliment to the loyalty of many millions, who make no effort to break through the wall of silence that Field Marshal Kitchener has erected between them and their army.

We know that England has declared war. In the papers we can read of the Red Cross societies, of funds patronized by the royal family for those who may be wounded, for those who may be left fatherless, for those who already have been left without support. No one need be a military expert to read in the streets signs of a nation at war, even though of those signs it would be improper to write. But in no paper in the United Kingdom will he learn that by land and sea British forces are engaged in the greatest war since their victory at Waterloo.

It makes the position of a correspondent somewhat difficult, but it shows that into this struggle of the giants England has entered without hysteria or vain boasting, but earnestly, calmly and undismayed.

New York Tribune
August 20, 1914

Davis Sure Germans Were Withdrawing

New York Tribune's Special Correspondent, at the Front in Belgium, Watched Operations of Large Body of French Troops Near Tirlemont

Brussels, Aug. 18, Noon (Delayed).—The censor allows the newspaper "Le Derniere Heure" this morning to state that shells are falling in Tirlemont and that a dozen houses are on fire.

Last night refugees from Tirlemont arrived here on the last train from that city. This morning they are coming in by motor cars. They left so suddenly that they have not even hand baggage. Their cars are repeatedly stopped and news of attack near Tirlemont is demanded, but their news is as scanty as their luggage and, like the stories of all who run away, exaggerated.

Yesterday I was close to Tirlemont with a column of French dragoons and artillery that was the rear guard of a large body of French forces. While not permitted to state what I saw, it was of a nature to thoroughly convince one that the Germans are withdrawing.

New York Tribune
August 23, 1914

Like a River of Steel It Flowed, Gray and Ghostlike

Brussels, Friday, Aug. 21, 2 P.M.—The entrance of the German army into Brussels has lost the human quality. It was lost as soon as the three soldiers who led the army bicycled into the Boulevard du Regent and asked the way to the Gare du Nord. When they passed the human note passed with them.

What came after them, and twenty-four hours later is still coming, is not men marching, but a force of nature like a tidal wave, an avalanche or a river flooding its banks. At this minute it is rolling through Brussels as the swollen waters of the Conemaugh Valley swept through Johnstown.

At the sight of the first few regiments of the enemy we were thrilled with interest. After they had passed three hours in one unbroken steel-gray column, we were bored. But when hour after hour passed and there was no halt, no breathing time, no open spaces in the ranks, the thing became uncanny, inhuman. You returned to watch it, fascinated. It held the mystery and menace of fog rolling toward you across the sea.

The gray of the uniforms worn by both officers and men helped this air of mystery. Only the sharpest eye could detect among the thousands that passed the slightest difference. All moved under a cloak of invisibility. Only after the most numerous and severe tests at all distances, with all materials and combinations of colors that give forth no color, could this gray have been discovered. That it was selected to clothe and disguise the German when he fights is typical of the German staff in striving for efficiency, to leave nothing to chance, to neglect no detail.

After you have seen this service uniform under conditions entirely opposite you are convinced that for the German soldier it is his strongest weapon. Even the most expert marksman cannot hit a target he cannot see. It is a gray green, not the blue gray of our Confederates. It is the gray of the hour just before daybreak, the gray of unpolished steel, of mist among green trees.

I saw it first in the Grand Palace in front of the Hotel de Ville. It was impossible to tell if in that noble square there was a regiment or a brigade. You saw only a fog that melted into the stones, blended with the ancient house fronts, that shifted and drifted, but left you nothing at which you could point.

Later, as the army passed below my window under the trees of the Botanical Park, it merged and was lost against the green leaves. It is no exaggeration to say that at a hundred yards you can see the horses on which the uhlans ride, but you cannot see the men who ride them.

If I appear to overemphasize this disguising uniform it is because of all the details of the German outfit it appealed to me as one of the most remarkable. The other day when I was with the rear guard of the French dragoons and cuirassiers and they threw out pickets, we could distinguish them against the yellow wheat or green gorse at half a mile, while these men passing in the street, when they have reached the next crossing, become merged into the gray of the paving stones and the earth swallows them. In comparison the yellow khaki of our own American army is about as invisible as the flag of Spain.

Yesterday Major General von Jarotsky, the German military governor of Brussels, assured Burgomaster Max that the German army would not occupy the city, but would pass through it. It is still passing. I have followed in campaigns six armies, but excepting not even our own, the Japanese, or the British, I have not seen one so thoroughly equipped. I am not speaking of the fighting qualities of any army, only of the equipment and organization. The German army moved into this city as smoothly and compactly as an Empire State Express. There were no halts, no open places, no stragglers.

This army has been on active service three weeks, and so far there is not apparently a chin strap or a horseshoe missing. It came in with the smoke pouring from cookstoves on wheels, and in an hour had set up post office wagons, from which mounted messengers galloped along the line of columns distributing letters, and at which soldiers posted picture postcards.

The infantry came in files of five, two hundred men to each company; the Lacers in coumns of four, with not a pennant missing. The quick-firing guns and fieldpieces were one hour at a time in passing, each gun with its caisson and ammunition wagon taking twenty seconds in which to pass.

The men of the infantry sang *Fatherland, My Fatherland*. Between each line of song they took three steps. At times two thousand men were singing in absolute rhythm and beat. When the melody gave way the silence was broken only by the same of iron-shod boots, and then again the song rose. When the singing ceased, the bands played marches. They were followed by the rumble of siege guns, the creaking of wheels, and of chains clanking against the cobblestones and the sharp, bell-like voices of the bugles.

For seven hours the army passed in such solid columns that not once might a taxicab or trolley car pass through the city. Like a river of steel it flowed, gray and ghostlike. Then, as dusk came and as thousands of horses' hoofs and thousands of iron boots continued to tramp forward they struck tiny sparks from the stones, but the horses and the men who beat out the sparks were invisible.

At midnight pack wagons and siege guns were still passing. At seven this morning I was awakened by the tramp of men and bands playing jauntily. Whether they marched all night or not I do not know, but now for twenty-six hours the gray army has rumbled by with the mystery of fog and the pertinacity of a steam roller.

New York Tribune
August 25, 1914

Germans Got Cold Cheer in Brussels

City Shut Up Like Clam at Approach of Army and Only a Few Hundred Curious Watched 26-Hour Passage of Troops

Brussels, Aug. 20 (delayed)—With the swiftness of moving pictures the scene here has changed to one of peace. Gone are smart officers of staff in front of the cafes, French and Belgian aviators in their fur jackets, the dust covered wounded, jubilant, shrieking motor horns and messengers on motorcycles. Now, following the instructions of the Burgomaster, the people have withdrawn indoors and the streets are strangely silent. Empty shops are closing, and taxicabs and automobiles, fearing seizure, have been secreted by their owners. When the Germans at last arrive—and three times this morning their approach has been heralded—their triumphal procession will be greeted coldly and by a very small audience.

Meanwhile the last train to Ostend, which had as many farewell appearances as Adelina Patti, finally departed and the station was closed. So also are the doors of the post office and the telegraph office, the latter closing instantly after I had deposited most of my money to pay cable tolls. For any cables the Germans will let us send we will need no money. Meanwhile, this dispatch is being taken to Ostend by motor car, but after the Germans enter that route may also be closed. The English correspondents and all the American correspondents except three got out last night. Two hundred Americans are registered at the American Legation.

The first Germans to enter Brussels were on bicycles and in gray, an officer and two privates. They were white with dust. Rifles were slung from their shoulders and their spiked helmets covered with khaki. At the circle where the Boulevard Regent meets the Chaussee de Louvain probably three hundred men and three or four women were gathered. They were, of course, of the concierge and workmen class in blouses. The windows of the houses in which they had been employed were so tightly closed that Lady Godiva might have ridden the length of the boulevard and felt no shame. Few people and hermetically closed house fronts made it appear as though within an hour the day had changed from Thursday to Sunday morning.

The entire route over which it was expected that the Germans would pass had been carefully policed. Both gendarmes and citizens with special licenses from the Burgomaster kept the few spectators back from the curb when the bicycles appeared. These same policemen forced those who advanced curiously to retreat. The Germans came riding quickly, obviously with no thought that they might be molested. One of them as he passed asked in French of a policeman the way to the railroad station. The man with the motor car to Ostend won't wait longer, so I must stop. The number of Germans immediately outside the city is reported to be about 16,000. They are to occupy the Royal Palace and the Hotel du Ville.

New York Tribune
August 31, 2014

Horrors of Louvain Told by Eyewitness; Circled Burning City

Vandalism and Atrocities on Women and Children Committed in Name of War, Says Richard Harding Davis

Officers Shot, Is German Excuse

Asserted that Burgomaster's Son Fired on Chief of Staff and Surgeons—Six-Hundred-Year-Old Town Turned Into a Wilderness

(Richard Harding Davis, the Tribune correspondent, was arrested as a spy and, after having been held for four days, was allowed to go. The dispatch below indicates that he was held in the train at Louvain during the burning of the town.)

I left Brussels on Thursday afternoon and have just arrived in London. For two hours on Thursday night I was in what for six hundred years had been the City of Louvain. The Germans were burning it, and to hide their work kept us locked in the railroad carriages. But the story as written against the sky was told to us by German soldiers incoherent with excesses; and we could read it in the faces of women and children being led to concentration camps and of citizens on their way to be shot.

The Germans sentenced Louvain on Wednesday to become a wilderness, and with the German system and love of thoroughness they left Louvain an empty, blackened shell. The reason for this appeal to the torch and the execution of non-combatants, as given to me on Thursday morning by General Von Lutwitz, military governor of Brussels, was this: On Wednesday while the German military commander of the troops in Louvain was at the Hotel de Ville talking to the burgomaster a son of the burgomaster with an automatic pistol shot the chief of staff and German staff surgeons.

Lutwitz claims this was the signal for the civil guard, in civilian clothes on roofs, to fire upon the German soldiers in the open square below. He said also the Belgians had quick-firing guns, brought from Antwerp. As for a week the Germans had occupied Louvain and closely guarded all approaches, the story that there was any gunrunning is absurd.

Fifty Germans were killed and wounded. For that, said Lutwitz, Louvain must be wiped out. So in pantomime with his fist he swept the papers across his table.

"The Hotel de Ville," he added, "was a beautiful building; it is a pity it must be destroyed."

Educated Many American Priests

Ten days ago I was in Louvain when it was occupied by Belgian troops and King Albert and his staff. The city dates from the eleventh century and the population was 42,000. The citizens were brewers, lacemakers, and manufacturers of ornaments for churches. The university once was the most celebrated in European cities, and still is, or was, headquarters of the Jesuits.

In the Louvain college many priests now in America have been educated, and ten days ago over the great yellow walls of the college I saw hanging two American flags. I found the city clean, sleepy and pretty, with narrow, twisting streets and smart shops and cafes set in glower gardens of the houses, with red roofs, green shutters and white walls.

Over those that faced south had been trained pear trees, their branches heavy with fruit spread out against the walls like branches of candelabra. The Town Hall was very old and very beautiful, an example of Gothic architecture, in detail and design more celebrated even than the Town Hall of Bruges or Brussels. It was five hundred years old, and lately had been repaired with great taste and at great cost.

Opposite was the Church of St. Pierre, dating from the fifteenth century, a very noble building, with many chapels filled with carvings of the time of the Renaissance in wood, stone and iron. In the university were 150,000 volumes.

Near it was the bronze statue of Father Damien, priest of the leper colony in the South Pacific, of which Robert Louis Stevenson wrote. All these buildings now are empty, exploded cartridges. Statues, pictures, carvings, parchments, archives—all are gone.

Compared with United States in Mexico

No one defends the sniper. But because ignorant Mexicans when their city was invaded fired upon our sailors, we did not destroy Vera Cruz. Even had we bombarded Vera Cruz, money could have restored it. Money can never restore Louvain. Great architects and artists, dead these six hundred years, made it beautiful, and their handiwork belonged to the world. With torch and dynamite the Germans have turned these masterpieces into ashes, and all the Kaiser's horses and all his men cannot bring them back again.

When by troop train we reached Louvain, the entire heart of the city was destroyed and fire had reached the Boulevard Tirlemont, which faces the railroad station. The night was windless, and the sparks rose in steady, leisurely pillars, falling back into the furnace from which they spread. In their work the soldiers were moving from the heart of the city to the outskirts, street by street, from house to house.

In each building, so German soldiers told me, they began at the first floor, and when that was burning steadily passed to the one next. There were no exceptions—whether it was a store, chapel or private residence it was destroyed. The occupants had been warned to go, and in each deserted shop or house the furniture was piled, the torch was stuck under it, and into the air went the savings of years, souvenirs of children, or parents, heirlooms that had passed from generation to generation.

The people had time only to fill a pillowcase and fly. Some were not so fortunate, and by thousands, like flocks of sheep, they were up and marched through the night to concentration camps. We were not allowed to speak to any citizen of Louvain, but the Germans crowded the windows, boastful, gloating, eager to interpret.

War on the Defenceless

We were free to move from one end of the train to the other, and in the two hours during which it circled the burning city war was before us in its most hateful aspect.

In other wars I have watched men on one hilltop, without haste, without heat, fire at men on another hill, and in consequence on both sides good men were wasted. But in those fights there were no women or children, and the shells struck only vacant stretches of veldt or uninhabited mountainsides.

At Louvain it was war upon the defenceless, war upon churches, colleges, shops of milliners and lacemakers; war brought to the bedside and the fireside, against women harvesting in the fields, against children in wooden shoes at play in the streets.

At Louvain that night the Germans were like men after an orgy.

There were fifty English prisoners, erect and soldierly. In the ocean of gray the little patch of khaki looked pitifully lonely, but they regarded the men who had outnumbered but not defeated them with calm bu uncurious eyes. In one way I was glad to see them there. Later they will bear witness as to how the enemy makes a wilderness and calls it war. It was a most weird picture.

On the high ground rose the broken spires of the Church of St. Pierre and the Hotel de Ville, and descending like steps were row beneath row of houses, roofless, with windows like blind eyes. The fire had reached the last row of houses, those on the Boulevard de Jodigne. Some of these were already cold, but others sent up steady, straight columns of flame. In others at the third and fourth stories the window curtains still hung, flowers still filled the window boxes, while on the first floor the torch had just passed and the flames were leaping. Fire had destroyed the electric plant, but at times the flames made the station so light that you could see the second hand of your watch, and again all was darkness, lit only by candles.

Men to be Shot Marched Past

You could tell when an officer passed by the electric torch he carried strapped to his chest. In the darkness the gray uniforms filled the station with an army of ghosts. You distinguished men only when pipes hanging from their teeth glowed red or their bayonets flashed.

Outside the station in the public square the people of Louvain passed in an unending procession, women bareheaded, weeping, men carrying the children asleep on their shoulders, all hemmed in by the shadowy army of gray wolves. Once they were halted, and among them were marched a line of men. They well knew their fellow townsmen. These were on their way to be shot. And better to point the moral an officer halted both processions and, climbing to a cart, explained why the men were to die. He warned others not to bring down upon themselves a like vengeance.

As those being led to spend the night in the fields looked across to those marked for death they saw old friends, neighbors of long standing, men of their own household. The officer bellowing at them from the cart was illuminated by the headlights of an automobile. He looked like an actor held in a spotlight on a darkened stage.

It was all like a scene upon the stage, so unreal, so inhuman, you felt it could not be true that the curtain of life, purring and crackling and sending up hot sparks to meet the kind, calm stars, was only a painted backdrop, that the reports of rifles from the dark rooms came from blank cartridges, and that these trembling shopkeepers and peasants, ringed in bayonets, would not in a few minutes really die, but that they themselves and their homes would be restored to their wives and children.

You felt it was only a nightmare, cruel and uncivilized. And then you remembered that the German Emperor has told us what it is. It is his Holy War.

New York Tribune
September 1, 1914

Germans Censor Notes of Envoys

Official Dispatches to Foreign Governments Blue Pencilled—Secretary Gibson, of American Legation, Sees Effect of Bombs Dropped in Belgium

London, Aug. 31.—After for one week closing the railroad from Brussels to Aix-la-Chapelle, the German military authorities reopened it on Thursday to carry the wounded and prisoners. For eight days Brussels had been isolated. The mail trains and telegraph were in the hands of the invaders.

They accepted our cables, censored them and three days later told us if we still wished it we could forward them. But only from Holland. By this they accomplished three things. They found out what we were writing, delayed for three days any news leaving the city and offered us an inducement to visit Holland, so ridding themselves of our presence.

The authorities were equally severe with the dispatches of those diplomats who still remained in Brussels. With the most chilly complacency they blue penciled official dispatches to foreign governments until the diplomats discovered what they were doing and sent cables in cipher, accompanied by open cables explaining to their ministers at home that their confidential messages were being censored and delayed in transmission.

Except by messenger on foot, there was no way to get news out of the city. If a motor car appeared it was at once commandeered. This was true also of horses and bicycles all over Brussels. You saw delivery wagons, private carriages, market carts with the shafts empty and the horse and harness gone. After three days a German soldier who did not own a bicycle was poor indeed.

Every Bicycle Seen Seized

Requisitions were given for these machines, stating they would be returned after the war, by which time they would be ready for the crap heap. Anyone on a bicycle outside the city was arrested, so the only way to get messages through was by going on foot to Ostend or Holland or by automobile for which the German authorities had given a special pass. As no one knew when one of these might start, we carried always with us our cables and letters and intrusted them to any stranger who was trying to run the lines.

Three out of four times the stranger would be arrested and ordered back to Brussels and our dispatches, with their news value departed, would be returned. I got one dispatch through only by subscribing heavily to the Belgian Red Cross fund, and sent an account of the Germans entering Brussels by an English boy, who, after being turned back three times, got through by night, and when he arrived in England his adventures were published in all the London papers. They made my story, for which he had taken the trip, extremely tame reading.

Hugh Gibson, secretary of the American Legation, was the first person in an official position to visit Antwerp after the Belgian government moved to that city, and even with his passes and flag flying from his automobile he reached Antwerp and returned to Brussels only after many delays and adventures. Not knowing the Belgians were advancing from the north, Gibson and his American flag were several times under fire, and on the days he chose for his excursion his route led him past burning towns and dead and wounded and between the lines of both forces actively engaged.

Carried Dispatches for Bryan

He was carrying dispatches from Brand Whitlock to Secretary Bryan. During the night he rested at Antwerp a Zeppelin airship passed over it, dropping one bomb at the end of the block in which Gibson was sleeping. He was awakened by the explosion and heard all of those that followed.

The next morning he was requested to accompany a committee appointed by the Belgian government to report upon the outrage, and he visited a house that had been wrecked and saw what was left of the bodies of those killed. People who were in the streets when the airship passed tell me it moved without any sound, as though the motor had been shut off and it was being propelled by momentum.

One bomb fell so near the palace where the Belgian Queen was sleeping as to destroy the glass in the windows and scar the walls. The bombs were large, containing smaller bombs of the size of shrapnel. Like shrapnel, on impact they scattered bullets over a radius of forty yards. One man who from a window on the eighth story of a hotel watched the airship pass says before each bomb fell that he saw electric torches signal from the roofs, as though giving directions as to where the bombs should fall.

The indignation of Americans as expressed in American newspapers at the airship attack upon innocent and sleeping non-combatants is greatly appreciated here. This morning all the London newspapers reprint editorials from our papers and make editorial comment.

I left Brussels on Thursday with Gerald Morgan, of the *Tribune*, and Will Irwin, of "Collier's," on the train carrying English prisoners and German wounded. In times of peace the trip to the German border lasts three hours, but we were in making it twenty-six hours, and, by order of the authorities, forbidden to leave the train.

Carriages with cushions were naturally reserved for the wounded, so we slept on wooden benches and on the floor. It was not possible to obtain food, and water was as scarce. At Graesbeek, ten miles from Brussels, we first saw houses on fire. They continued with us to Liege. Village after village had been completely wrecked, and at Saventhen. Louvain, Tirlemont and Liege the destruction was the more appalling because more extended. In his march to the sea Sherman lived on the country. He did not destroy it, and as against the burning of Columbia must be placed to the discredit of the Germans the wiping out of an entire countryside.

Peasants Flee Burning Homes

For many miles we saw procession after procession of peasants fleeing from one burning village, which had been their home, to other villages, to find only blackened walls and smouldering ashes. In no part of Northern Europe is there a countryside fairer than that between Aix-la-Chapelle and Brussels, but the Germans have made of it a graveyard. It looks as though a cyclone had uprooted its houses, gardens and orchards and a prairie fire had followed.

When we reached Holland, in view of what had befallen Belgium, I was not surprised to find the people leaning strongly toward a policy of friendship with Germany. Mobilization was going forward briskly, and it was pitiful to see the honest, eager faces of recruits, ignorant of what was before them crowding the troop trains. But their officers did not know on which side they were to fight. Their sympathies drew them toward England; their fears may force them to support Germany.

New York Tribune
September 2, 1914

Tells Experience as War Prisoner

Richard Harding Davis Gives His Opinion of the German Campaign in Belgium, as Witnessed and Heard of While He Was a Captive

London, Sept. 13—I have not seen the text of the letter addressed by President Wilson to Americans urging them to preserve toward this war the mental attitude of neutrals. But I have seen the war. I feel very deeply, therefore, that if I did not earnestly try to convince Americans that they should be neutrals I should be shirking a responsibility

Were the conflict in Belgium a fair fight on equal terms between man and man, then without question the duty of Americans would be to keep to the sidelines and preserve open minds. But it is not a fair fight.

Germany is fighting foully. She is defying not only the rules of war but all rules of humanity

If public opinion is to help in preventing further outrages by her forces and in hastening this unspeakable conflict to a close, it should be directed against those who offend. If we are convinced that one opponent is fighting honestly and that his adversary is striking below the belt or gouging and biting, then for us to maintain a neutral attitude of mind is unworthy and the attitude of a coward.

When a mad dog runs amuck in a village it is the duty of every farmer to get his gun and destroy it, not to lock himself indoors and preserve toward the dog and those who face him a neutral mind.

This is not a war against Germans, as we know Germans in America who are among our sanest and most industrious and most responsible fellow countrymen. It is a war, as Winston Churchill in his interview last Sunday explained, against the military aristocracy of Germany, men who are six hundred years behind the times; who, to preserve their class against democracy, have perverted every great invention of modern times to the uses of warfare, to the destruction of life.

These men are military mad. Their idea of government is as far opposed to our own as is martial law and the free speech of our own meetings. Every belief of these high-born butchers is opposed to every principle that is to us most dear.

If they will make of Europe an armed camp, they will control commerce on the seas; they will either destroy our commerce with Europe or dictate as to what goods they will admit, or admit them on their own terms.

Meanwhile they are destroying Belgium, a country with which they had no quarrel. The land they have devastated was not waste land, sparsely settled and uninhabited. it was the oldest and most closely built up countryside in Europe. The villages, towns and cities touch with their skirts the skirts of the next adjoining place. They run as close together as do The Bronx, Larchmont, Rye and New Rochelle. The cities they have destroyed with bombs and fire are cities like Rochester, Utica and Troy. These cities were not fortified. They were industrial centers, and, besides, possessed treasures of art and architecture that belonged not alone to the Belgians but to the world.

I have seen Germans at work. For a time I was a prisoner and forced to march with them, and the destruction they wrought was not the havoc that war always brings.

In six other wars all I have seen that was outrageous was not so terrible, so unnecessary, so wanton, as the outrages of the German army in the short distance between Brussels and Liege.

The allies asked of the Belgians to hold back the invaders only for two day. They held them back for fifteen. It is for that they are being punished, not because the townspeople are firing upon the Germans. No one who has been in Belgium this last month believes that charge.

I passed on foot through many villages, and in all read the proclamations issued by the burgomaster, commanding the people to turn over to him every firearm in their possession, and the date of each of these proclamations antedated the entry of the Germans. The Germans were the aggressors. They approached non-combatants always gun in hand.

Again and again have I been told the same story by Belgian shopkeepers and the proprietors of cafes and hotels. "They put a gun at my head." "Why?" I asked, and the Belgian would shrug his shoulders and say, "Because they wanted eggs or a note changed, or a bed. But why shoot me for so small a matter as a couple of eggs?"

My own experiences were the same. They never demanded my papers without first sticking an automatic pistol in my face. Once, when I was seated by the road engaged in eating a sandwich, five of them rushed at me from the rear, each waving an automatic pistol. They seemed to me like men on the verge of hysteria, officers and privates alike.

When I was a prisoner with them, one of their own aeroplanes passed over us. They thought it an English machine, and Count von Schwerin, commanding the 7th Division, and all his staff at the same time began shrieking commands, some to shoot, others not to shoot. They were like men suddenly gone crazy. It was a most pitiable exhibition.

Their conduct throughout can be explained in only one way. They are men who know they are in the wrong, that their cause is unlawful; and like a man who enters a house as a burglar, they do not hesitate at murder. In no other way can you explain their casting floating mines among innocent fishermen, their dropping bombs from airships upon sleeping women, their wrecking churches, universities and libraries and their execution of non-combatants.

In comparison, let me relate one incident to illustrate how the plucky Belgian wages war. When our secretary of the legation at Brussels, Hugh Gibson, returned from Brussels to Antwerp, which was the day after the zeppelin had hurled her bombs into that city, the Belgian government gave him a package to be delivered to the German governor of Brussels. It had nothing at all to do with the Germans' infernal machine, but contained letters of German prisoners in Antwerp, which the Belgians were forwarding for them to their wives and children. Belgians do not wage war on women, nor do their allies.

Between them and the Germans, one who has seen what I have seen at Louvain, Tirlemont and Liege finds it hard to preserve an attitude of mind correctly neutral.

New York Tribune
September 4, 1914

Eight American Writers Arrested

Tribune Correspondent Cables Account of His Capture by Germans and How He Was Saved from Being Shot as English Officer

This war has been the end of war correspondents. Of several, that came near being true in every sense of the word. The trouble was that, unable to obtain credentials, they tried without them to see the fighting, and in consequence were arrested.

No prejudices or favouritism was shown. Every army in turn arrested every correspondent. I was arrested by the Belgians, the French, the Germans, and even by the Dutch. But by the time we reached Holland I was so sick for sleep that all I remember of that journey is Gerald Morgan dragging me out of the railroad carriage, handing me my tickets and shaking me into wakefulness. When we reached the gangplank of the English boat at Flushing he exclaimed, "Thank God, we're now free from arrest." I asked, "Have we been arrested?" "For two days," said Gerald, "you were taken across Holland by that gendarme who carried your valise."

Throughout my broken slumbers I had thought the gendarme was a railroad porter, and it had struck me as curious that in Holland all railroad porters looked exactly alike.

The American correspondent who first scored an arrest was Captain Granville Fortescue, who lives in Washington, and who, during President Roosevelt's administration, was military aide at the White House. He served in the Cuban war with the Roosevelt rough riders, and rose to the rank of captain in the regular army. With the Japanese army in front of Port

Arthur he was our military attaché. When the present war started, Fortescue and his family were in Brussels. He was the first man to see any fighting and get his stories back to New York.

With the Belgian army he was very popular and, banking on this, when the French arrived at Namur Captain Fortescue walked to meet the French general, saying genially to him: "Welcome to our city." To this the French general answered: "Who the devil are you?"

And, not being satisfied with Fortescue's reply, the general, in accordance with the rules that the French War Office has laid down, ordered him to Paris under arrest.

Fortescue protested that all his clothes were in his apartments in Brussels, and asked that he be permitted to return to that city, giving his word of honor to send out no information concerning what he had seen. At the expression, "word of honor," the French general injudiciously sniffed. Even more injudiciously Fortescue then told him that he wanted him to know that his word of honor was as good as that of any general in France.

But the last word went to the general. It was, "You are under arrest." Fortescue replied, "You are on Belgian territory and cannot arrest me." "Then," said the general, "I will arrest you on French territory." And surrounded by French bayonets Fortescue was marched across the border.

Legally arrested and for three days locked up in the scullery of a roadside inn, he was then taken by plainclothes men to Paris and led before the chief of police, who said a mistake had been made and offered to give Fortescue an ample apology. Not being able to clothe himself in an apology, Fortescue returned to London to refit. He arrived there with no heavier luggage than a pair of military hairbrushes.

On August 17 four more American correspondents fell into the advancing tidal wave of Germans. Their intention was only to paddle in the fringe of the wave, but it moved too quickly. They were John T. McCutcheon, of all our cartoonists if not the foremost certainly the most human; genial Irvin Cobb, a rival humorist, representing "The Saturday Evening Post"; Will Irwin, of "Collier's Weekly," and Arno Dosch, a Socialist of the Harvard school, representing "World's Work."

In a taxicab they went from Brussels to within three kilometres of Louvain, where the chauffeur refused to venture further. But he promised to wait for them while they visited the city on foot. They arrived in the public square of Louvain, which a week later was reduced to ruins, and, at the invitation of a Jesuit priest, who had visited America, sat in front of a cafe and refreshed themselves. Suddenly six Belgian soldiers ran past them, and at the entrance to the square they saw Uhlans in pursuit.

Led by McCutcheon, experienced in many wars, they retreated in good order in the direction of the taxicab, only to find that the taxicab driver had not waited to collect his fare, and, also in good order, was falling rapidly back upon Brussels.

Rising like gray ghosts from the wheat fields was a skirmish line of Uhlans. They paused; there was a hurried change of tactics, and, under fire both from Belgians and Germans, they returned to Louvain. There they surrendered themselves to the officer in command. They explained that they were American correspondents who had lost touch with their transport.

"But," said the German officer, "correspondents are not permitted with the German army." "We know that," said Cobb, "but here we are. What are you going to do about it?"

The German answered by placing them under detention in their hotel, in front of which for three days they sat around little iron tables playing dominos and watching miserable Belgian citizens led past them to execution. Undismayed by this experience, which caused them to miss the entrance of the German army into Brussels, on August 23 they again set forth to seek other adventures, their numbers now increased by the presence of John O'Connell Bennett, the "Chicago Tribune's" former dramatic critic; Harry Hanson, of "The Chicago Daily News"; Lewis, of the Associated Press, and Maurice Gerbault, of "The Chicago Daily News." Irwin and Dosch next day returned to Brussels, bringing word that Gerbault had been taken by the Germans as a suspected spy, chiefly on account of his nationality, and also because, against all our warnings, he would insist on taking photographs, which by every army in this war is forbidden.

When I left Brussels on August 20 these correspondents had completely disappeared, until this morning, when a telegram arrived from Hanson, dated from Brussels.

The others are probably with him, but wherever they may be they are safe. Dosch and Irwin, who came back, report that Cobb, who is of heavy proportions, was arrested by all the Germans entirely as a humorist. He can take a joke as well as make one, and wherever they went all the villagers lined the streets, and their laughter shook the tiled roofs.

His clothes having failed him, Cobb had remodelized in the garb of a Belgian peasant, and his appearance filled all who saw him with delight. Secretly, he was unhappy because he carried on his person much gold, to which he objected strongly on account of its weight. When last seen by Irwin, he was threatening, rather than carry the rich man's burden further, to throw it into the next wheat field.

The fact that word of him has not reached London need cause no anxiety. By this time he and his companions have returned to Brussels, or, like Hanson, have crossed the border to Holland. But even should they wish to communicate their safe arrival, there is no way by which they could get word out of Belgium. Communication is at present shut off even from our American Minister, Brand Whitlock. He is both an admirer and friend of Cobb and McCutcheon and may be relied upon to guard their interests in the same manner in which, since the war began, he has protected and assisted every American who has applied to him for aid. Incidentally, the administration is to be congratulated in having at this crisis a minister in Belgium as efficient as the distinguished ex-mayor of Toledo, and a representative as experienced in diplomacy as his secretary, Hugh Gibson. They form a working team which could not be improved upon.

Starts Out to See Some Fighting

My own experience with the Germans was most disagreeable. It was danger without excitement, adventure without one pleasant thrill. It was reported in Brussels, on August 23, that the night before there had been fighting at Hal, a town ten miles from the city, and that the French were advancing from Enghien, a town ten miles further south. With Gerald Morgan, I drove to Hal, and finding there had been no fighting there, continued on foot toward Enghien. We kept to the main road, down which the German army, commanded by General von Kluck, accompanied by the Grand Duke of Holstein, was proceeding in unbroken column. They had frequently stopped us, but as our papers gave us permission to visit the environs of Brussels, always allowed us to continue.

We appreciated that the environs could not stretch much further than Hal, and that at any moment some officer also would appreciate that fact and order us back. Morgan very wisely decided to return before he was sent back under guard. I continued on foot to Enghien, spent the night there, and at 6 the next morning started south, hoping when the German column finally clashed with the French to be present. I made no effort to conceal my papers, and walked with the column when asked concerning my papers, and talking freely with the officers.

I thought I was on the road to Soignies, but to embarrass the Germans the Belgians had destroyed the signposts, and by mistake I took the road to Ath. This for me was unfortunate, as it was down this road that a German army corps was being sent at doublequick to strike the British left. The success of this maneuver depended upon secrecy, and as soon as I appeared I was placed in the ranks of an infantry company and told that I must remain with it until the general commanding examined my papers.

Was Kept At "Double-Quick" Five Hours.

For five hours we marched at double-quick, and from that and the obvious excitement of the officers, I saw that they were planning a surprise. About noon I was placed in an automobile and sent forward to where Count de Schweren, commanding the seventh division, was seated by the roadside with his staff. They examined my papers and pointed out that I was far outside the limits that my pass permitted me to go.

From the circumstance that my passport had been made out in London and that the photograph affixed to it showed me in khaki uniform, they decided that I was an English officer detailed as a spy, and that when captured I was endeavouring to get through their lines to Tournai and warn the English of the flanking movement, which, it was hoped, would surprise them and roll up their left flank upon the French centre. I explained that our army regulations required war correspondents to appear in khaki, and asked if they supposed that our ambassador in London would issue a passport to an English officer. They replied that it would be easy for an English officer to deceive the ambassador.

I then urged that I had seen no more than everyone in Brussels for the last four days had seen in the streets. "You have seen enough in this road," the chief of staff said, pointing to the officers of the staff, "to explain what we are trying to accomplish. It is enough to justify us in shooting you now."

Gets Third Degree From German Generals.

Fortunately, General de Schweren decided that the matter was of such importance that it must be brought before his superior officer, the general commanding the army corps.

They said they would not reach him until midnight, and the chief of staff assured me that the highest general would then surely order me shot. All of the staff spoke English, and in turn put me through the third degree. After consulting together, they would again come at me with fresh questions, intended to trap and confuse. This cross examination lasted three hours.

Some were convinced that I was an American, who, through ignorance, had stumbled upon their secret. Others argued that the possession of the secret was the only point to be considered, and that to protect themselves I must be put out of the way. It was all as cold blooded as a game of bridge.

I had to do a lot of thinking, and to think very fast. I offered to pay 500 francs to any peasant they would send on a bicycle to Brussels with a note from me to Brand Whitlock. I wrote a note to him, which I intended they should read, in which I addressed him in terms which apparently proved we were very old friends. As a matter of fact, I had met him only since coming to Brussels. But I knew he would understand. I offered that, if within five hours the American minister did not come for me in his own automobile and prove the truth of my story, they could, instead of waiting until midnight, then take me out and shoot me, thus relieving themselves of my presence by five hours.

He Takes a Chance On His Life

As I hoped, they opened the letter and apparently were impressed by it. In any event, it created what lawyers call a stay of proceedings.

They continued to take me south in automobiles, passing me on from one officer to another, until we reached a little town called Ligne. There they locked me in a room with a stone floor and stone walls, apparently built for the purpose. Into this they threw bundles of wheat, and placed a guard at the door, ordering me to keep it open. Every time I moved that sentry raised his automatic.

I worked out a plan which I hoped would act as a sort of injunction. It was that they should return me to Brussels by the shortest route, that if I were found off that route I was to be shot, and that unless within two days I reported to the military governor of Brussels, I was to be shot.

I outlined this plan to Major Alfred Wirth, who lives in Bernburg, on the Saale River. He was friendly toward me, but apparently thought I had little chance, as, whenever he visited my room and sat down beside me on the stones, his eyes would fill with tears. That was discouraging, but his feelings certainly led him to aid me.

At 10 o'clock an electric torch, strapped to the chest of an officer, flashed in my eyes and woke me. The officer ordered me to accompany him at once to the commanding general.

His manner persuaded me that the general had decided against me. We drove to a beautiful chateau, set far back in a magnificent park. It was filled with officers, and automobiles were coming and going at great speed. I heard them say, "The English are coming." And their manner toward me now became even more unfriendly.

A Lift in An Auto Saves Him

After an hour the chief of staff brought me my papers and my knapsack and told me that, under certain conditions, I was free. The conditions were those I had outlined to my friend, Major Wirth. He had carried them to the general. There is no question but that it is due to his offices I was not left lying in a field.

The passport given me ordered me to proceed by a stated route to Brussels. The distance was fifty miles, and as it was necessary to walk, they calculated on my making twenty-five miles a day. The pass stated that unless I reported by midnight on August 26, I was to be shot as a spy.

I started back at 3 that morning, but in the darkness was challenged so often that, although time was precious, it seemed wiser to delay until day came. Then, when it was light, I had walked to beyond Ath, when by a most fortunate stroke of good luck, I obtained a seat in an automobile in which a kindly old German general was going to Brussels.

On arriving, instead of reporting to the military governor, I at once reported to Brand Whitlock, and he instantly conveyed me, unwashed and undusted, to the Hotel de Ville.

There he explained that I was reporting not because the pass ordered me to report, but in spite of that fact. And he demanded that from the pass the word spy be removed.

They accordingly wrote upon the pass that I was a friend of the American minister, and a correspondent well known to him, and that I was no spy. To that they affixed the seal of the German government.

It was a very close call.

New York Tribune
September 4, 1914

Says Kaiser, Breaking Word, Tricked Czar

Story Related by Grand Duke Alexander of How German Emperor Gave Promise as "Soldier" Not to Mobilize

London, Sept. 3—A interesting story, in which the Grand Duke Alexander Michaelovitch, brother-in-law of the Czar, charges the German emperor with duplicity and trickery of the most surprising nature, has come to me from Barclay H. Warburton, of Philadelphia, who arrived here on Monday from the newly christened city of Petrograd. Mr. Warburton is extremely well known at home, as for years he was the proprietor of "The Philadelphia Evening Telegraph," which newspaper he lately sold to his brother-in-law, Rodman Wanamaker, who, until the war came, was financing the transatlantic flight of Lieutenant Porte.

Of late years Mr. Warburton has interested himself in the sale of the Lewis automatic gun, the invention of an American officer. This gun and other war material he has sold to the Russian government. He is well known in Russia, and is the personal friend of Grand Duke Alexander, who, on his visit to America last summer, was Mr. Warburton's guest. The story in Mr. Warburton's own words is as follows:

"A few days before I left St. Petersburg the Grand Duke Alexander, who, by his marriage to the Grand Duchess Xenia, is a brother-in-law of the Czar, came to that city to take command of his regiment. At his palace on the Moika he told me that shortly before war broke out, when both the Russian and German armies were mobilizing, the German Emperor telegraphed the Czar a personal message, in which he offered, if Russia would cease her mobilization of the army, to stop mobilizing his own.

Pledged Word as "Soldier"

" 'I promise,' the message ran, 'on the word of a soldier.'

"On the strength of this the Czar instructed Soukhomlinoff, his minister of war, that he wished all movements of troops at once to cease. The minister of war expressed his doubts regarding the honesty of the German emperor, but the Czar pointed out that the Kaiser's message was a personal assurance, and insisted that mobilization cease. Eight hours later, after the Russian mobilization had been entirely halted, the Czar learned from his embassy in Berlin that, according to orders issued by the German emperor himself, efforts to quickly mobilize the German army had been redoubled.

" 'This,' the Grand Duke said, 'was told me this morning by the Czar. It is only too evident that my brother-in-law was tricked by the German emperor.'

" 'It is bad enough,' the Grand Duke said, 'to break the word of an emperor, but William broke the word of a soldier.'

"August 2 Soukhomlinoff himself, not knowing that I had heard this story from the Grand Duke Alexander, told me exactly the same story, only adding that from the first he believed that the German emperor, by a dishonest trick, was trying to gain time."

Mr. Warburton says that the Russians charge German with fomenting and financing the labor riots that occurred in St. Petersburg the week before the war. They claim to have evidence showing that two million marks were furnished to the revolutionists by Germany and that all the ringleaders of the riots were found to be Germans.

Relied on Ulster Difficulty

They believe that Germany thought that with the Ulster difficulty England would be at a great handicap and that Russia, also occupied with labor troubles at home and fearing a revolution, would not dare to enter the field. This would leave France without allies. But as soon as war was declared all internal dissensions in St. Petersburg ended.

Men who had hooted at officers now knelt to kiss their hands, and all classes showed the most splendid spirit. The civic demonstrations were remarkable, thousands of persons marching through the streets bare-headed carrying portraits of the Czar and at each second street kneeling to pray.

The government has purchased all autocars and commandeered all cab and bus horses. The most absolute conspiracy of silence conceals all military movements. Telegrams from officers in the field are limited to three words: "Am well; love." Each of these is first sent to a clearing house, and from there relayed, so that no wife in Russia may know where is her husband or his regiment.

Mr. Warburton is very happy over some successful gun running. Word that war was inevitable reached him in Paris on July 25 from the Russians, who ordered him to rush all the stock he had on hand. His guns, light mitrailleuses, weighing twenty-five pounds and used in aeroplanes, were in Birmingham. He brought them to London by motor truck and placed them in steamer trunks on which were painted different initials, coronets and names of cities. His mechanicians claimed these trunks, and in bond had them conveyed safely across German into Russia on the last Nord express.

A day later the railroad tracks leading into Germany were deserted, but the guns were safely in Russia. That was the last lot of Lewis guns to leave England, where the factory is now supplying them only to the British War Office.

When I asked Mr. Warburton where the Russian armies are now he said: "I do not know where they are today, but in three weeks they will be marching down Unter den Linden."

New York Tribune
September 15, 1914

Paris Standing Strain of War Complacently

Paris, Sept. 14. – Those who fled from Paris described it as a city doomed as a waste place, desolate as a graveyard. Those who run away always are alarmists. They are defensive. They must explain why they ran away.

Paris is like one of those Newport palaces out of season. The owners have temporarily closed it; the windows are barred, the furniture and paintings draped in linen, a caretaker and a night watchman are in possession. It is an old saying that all good Americans go to Paris when they die. Most of them take no chances and prefer to visit it while they are alive.

Before this war, if the visitor was disappointed, it was the fault of the visitor, not of Paris. She was all things to all men. To some she offered triumphal arches, statues, paintings; to others by day racing and by night Maxims and the Rat Mort. Some loved her for the bookstalls along the Seine and ateliers of the Latin Quarter; some for her parks, forest, gardens and boulevards; some because of the Luxembourg; some only as a place where everybody was smiling, happy and polite, where they were never bored, where they were always young, where the lights never went out and there was no early call. Should they today revisit her they would find her grown grave and decorous and going to bed at sundown, but still smiling bravely, still polite.

Great Emptiness in Streets

You cannot wipe out Paris by removing even two million people and closing Cartiers and the Café de Paris.

There still remain some hundred miles of boulevards, the Seine and her bridges, the Arc de Triomphe, with the sun setting behind it and the Gardens of the Tuileries. You cannot send them to the storehouse or wrap them in linen. And the spirit of the people of Paris you cannot crush nor stampede.

Between Paris two months since and Paris today the most striking difference is lack of population. Idle rich, the employees of the government and tourists of all countries are missing. They leave a great emptiness when you walk the streets. You feel either that you are up very early before any one is awake or that you are in boom town from which the boom had departed. Rue de la Paix and the boulevards are as empty as Wall Street on a legal holiday.

On almost every one of the noted shops "Ferme" is written large or it has been turned over to the use of the Red Cross. Of the smaller shops that remain open are chiefly bakeshops and chemists, but no man need go naked or hungry. In every block he will find at least one place where he can be clothed and fed. But the theatres are all closed. No one is in a mood to laugh, and certainly no one wishes to consider anything more serious than the present crisis. So there are no revues, operas or comedies.

The Theatre Francais, which in the war of 1870 remained open, is closed, and the Nouveau Cirque, where "Chocolat," the black "Marceline" of Paris used to disport in the water, is now a hospital.

Chicken Dinners Come High

There is just enough of everything, as the English say, to go on with. There are just enough taxicabs and fiacres, just enough restaurants, three in all; just enough hotels. In my hotel I am a solitary guest. I know of two others where American friends each occupy the same enviable position. The proprietors are glad to have even one patron. I occupy a suite in the Hotel de l'Empire from which Eugenie, when she became an empress, moved to the Tuileries.

It costs eight francs a day. But should I want chicken for dinner it would cost me 12 francs. If I wanted rolls I could not have them, for *petit pain* consumes too much flour, and so all bread is now baked in large loaves. Everywhere possible the service is rendered by women. When yesterday I arrived at 4 o'clock in the morning women were acting as street cleaners, dragging across the boulevards the snake-like hose on wheels. There are women even on the tram cars as conductors. Men not strong enough for the campaign are in the civil government in every capacity. A man not in uniform wears a brassard on his arm, which shows he is a postman, fireman or messenger.

As in Brussels and London, Boy Scouts are filling positions as messengers, clerks and watchmen once held by their seniors. To offset the empty streets there is the splendid color in thousands of flags. For miles you see from every house a flag of France or the grouped flags of the Allies. They give to the city a brilliant holiday air, as though for some great procession she had decked herself.

Of all the many uniforms the most picturesque are those of the native soldiers of Algiers and Morocco, the Turcos and Zoaves, swaggering in red fez and baggy breeches. They are splendid and soldierly looking. It is no wonder the Germans object to them in this war. I would want them kept out of any war in which they are not on my side. They and the English in khaki always are surrounded by crowds, and when they move on to tell their tale to a fresh audience the crowd cheers them.

Also it cheered this morning when a motorcar slowly rolled down the Boulevard Capucines, bearing aloft two German standards. The soldier who had single-handedly captured one of them was given the *medaille militaire*, the highest military honor. But an hour later, when two wounded men raced by in an automobile, each wearing a German spiked helmet, people only smiled.

They know that to own a helmet you do not necessarily have to fight for it, and that as souvenirs they command a high price. On the contrary, owing to the scarcity of money, in order to get it people ask less than usual. As, for example, my imperial suite at $1.60 a day. In days of peace it would be many times that.

The Great Change is at Night

The great change that has come over Paris is wrought at 8 o'clock each night. Then, at the hour when once she began to blaze forth in all her brilliancy, she goes to sleep, or, if she does not sleep, she lies awake in the darkness. It is darkness so profound that on the Avenue Champs Elysees you feel as though lost in a great forest. It is not a pleasant sensation. It is not that you are afraid you will be waylaid and robbed, but rather that you yourself are intent upon some burglary. The lamps of your cab are the only ones in sight, and the sound of your footsteps echo loudly. You feel like an "Apache" bent upon a predatory errand.

So, finding not after 9 o'clock a single light burning in a café and those of the street lamps only at great distances like lighthouses, you are forced indoors. And so is everyone else, and by 10 o'clock Paris, the gay, wicked and beautiful, is as dark as a fishing village on Cape Cod and asleep. And as she sleeps, like the arms of a mother over a cradle, above her rooftops the great searchlights pass in slow, protecting, majestic gestures.

New York Tribune
September 15, 1914

Public Opinion Ends Aero Visits

Richard Harding Davis Believes Germans Heard of Ambassador Herrick's Questioning of Paris Police

Paris, Sept. 14. – The retreat of the German right, which on September 6 was as near to Paris as the Forest of Crecy, to points seventy kilometers distant has naturally relieved the tension in this city. It has also cleared the air of aeroplanes. Now for airships to reach the city it would be necessary to pass over the heads of the allied armies.

But it is also probable that public opinion has much to do in calling a halt to this visit from which only the innocent were sufferers. Acting on the protest of the American Committee in Paris, Ambassador Herrick asked the police for evidence of bomb throwing from aeroplanes. The fact that this request was made probably became known to the German authorities in Berlin.
In any event, for six days the aeroplanes' visits have ceased. In buildings of historic value that could not be replaced, in monuments and galleries of art, Paris is so rich that to throw a bomb without destroying something of value to the world would require a careful aim. Those bombs that did fall were of specially vicious nature. I saw a photograph, taken by the authorities, of the body of a young woman who was struck by a bomb. It showed nineteen wounds. The mutilations of other bodies could not be described.

German Position Made Untenable

During the withdrawal of the Germans the question was raised if it were not voluntary and part of a preconceived plan to strengthen the army in the center. There is evidence now on the battlefields over which General von Kluck's army retreated to show that the positions the Germans attempted to hold were rendered untenable. On the hills where their guns were entrenched Normandy poplars of enormous girth and height were uprooted by the English artillery as by a cyclone, and where trees cannot stand neither can men.

A further evidence was the amount of ammunition abandoned by the Germans. Apparently no effort had been made to save it. This and the number of dead still lying in the fields and in the trenches suggest it was not a withdrawal according to a plan, but a forced flight. Still further proof of this is the guns taken by the British.

Prisoners Lost Through Error

The prisoners they captured are said to have been lost through the error of their own people, who too soon blew up the bridges across the Marne, thinking that all their men already had crossed. About fifteen hundred who had not crossed the river were swiftly surrounded by the British and surrendered.

The rule against permitting correspondents to accompany the allied armies was today again illustrated by the return to Paris under arrest of John Reed, of "The Metropolitan Magazine"; Mr. Boone, of "The Times"; Mr. Jeffries, of "The Daily Mail"; Robert Dunn of "The New York Evening Post," and two others of "The Daily Mirror" and "The Times." Two days ago the six walked from Crecy to Coulommiers and asked permission of General Smith Dorrien to accompany his column. They were by him turned over to the French staff, who explained that they were not under arrest, but sent them guarded by gendarmes to Paris, with orders to report at 5 o'clock to-day at military headquarters and then proceed to the City of Tours, where they are to be released. On their papers they are described as "not dangerous."

Whether the trip to Tours is intended as a punishment or is meant to keep them well away from the field of operations they do not know. They departed for that city this evening.

New York Tribune
September 22, 1914

Vivid Description of the Shelling of Rheims Cathedral

Statues and Carvings, Collected Through the Centuries, Representing Angels, Apostles and Patriarchs, are Now Piles of Junk

Wounded Germans, Attended by French Red Cross Doctors, Are Slain by Shells from Guns of Their Own Comrades

Paris, Sept. 19.—In several ways the city of Rheims is celebrated. Some know her only through her cathedral, where were crowned all but six of the kings of France, and where the stained glass windows, with those in the cathedrals of Chartres and Burgos, Spain, are the most beautiful in all the world. Children know Rheims through the wicked magpie which the archbishop excommunicated; and to their elders, if they are rich. Rheims is the place from which comes all their champagne.

On September 4 the Germans entered Rheims and occupied it until the 17th, when they retreated to the hills north of the city, without fighting. But the day before yesterday the French forces, having entered Rheims, the Germans bombarded the city with field guns and howitzers. Rheims is fifty-six miles from Paris, but though I started at an early hour, so many bridges have been blown up that I did not reach Rheims until 3 o'clock in the afternoon. At that hour the French artillery, to the east at Nogent and immediately outside the northern edge of the town, were firing on the German positions and the Germans were replying, many of their shells falling in the heart of the city.

Damage is Called Intentional

The proportion of those that struck the cathedral or houses within a hundred yards of it to those falling on other buildings was about six to one. So what damage the cathedral suffered was from blows delivered not by accident, but with intent. As the priests put it, firing on the church was "*expres*" (of set purpose).

The cathedral dominates not only the city but the countryside. It rises from the plain as Gibralter rises from the sea, as the pyramids rise from the desert. And at a distance of six miles, as you approach from Paris along the valley of the Marne, it has more the appearance of a fortress than a church. But when you stand in the square beneath and look up, it is entirely ecclesiastic, of noble and magnificent proportions, in design inspired, much too sublime for the kings it has crowned, and almost worthy of the king in whose honor seven hundred years ago it was reared. It has been called "perhaps the most beautiful structure produced in the Middle Ages." On the west façade rising tier upon tier are 560 statues and carvings. The statues are of angels, martyrs, patriarchs, apostles, the vices and virtues, the Virgin and Child. In the centre of these is the famous rose window; on either side giant towers.

At my feet down the steps leading to the three portals were pools of blood. There was a priest in the square, a young man with white hair and with a face as strong as one of those of the saints carved in stone, and as gentle. He was *curé doyen* of the cathedral, Canon Frezet, and he explained the pools of blood. Before they retreated the Germans had carried their wounded up the steps into the nave of the cathedral, had spread straw upon the stone flagging, placed with it a bucket of water and a raw shoulder of beef and abandoned to the care of the enemy those unfortunates who had become a burden. In this procedure there was nothing exceptional. During this last week of retreat it has been their rule. Along the twenty miles of their withdrawal the wake of the Germans is strewn with these derelicts, no longer able to help them, no longer able to help themselves.

The curé guided me to the side door, unlocked it and led the way into the cathedral. It is built in the form of a crucifix, and so vast is the edifice that many chapels are lost in it and the lower half is in a shadow. But from high above the stained windows of the thirteenth century, or what was left of them, was cast a glow so gorgeous, so wonderful, so pure, that it seemed to come direct from the other world.

German Shell Kills German Wounded

From north and south the windows shed a radiance of deep blue, like the blue of the sky by moonlight on the coldest night of winter, and from the west the great rose window glowed with the warmth and beauty of a thousand rubies. Beneath it, bathed in crimson light, where for generations French men and women have knelt in prayer, where Joan of Arc helped place the crown on Charles VII, was piled three feet of dirty straw, and on the straw were gray-coated Germans, covered with the mud of the fields, caked with blood, white and haggard from the loss of it, from the lack of sleep, rest and food. The entire west end of the cathedral looked like a stable, and in the blue and purple rays from the gorgeous windows the wounded were as unreal as ghosts. Already two of them had passed into the world of ghosts. They had not died from their wounds, but from a shell sent by their own people.

It had come screaming into this backwater of war and tearing out leaded window panes as you would destroy cobwebs, and had burst among those who already had paid the penalty. And so two of them, done with pack drill, goose step, half rations and forced marches, lay under straw the priests had heaped upon them. The toes of their boots pointed grotesquely upward. Their gray hands were clasped rigidly as though in prayer.

Fate of German Soldiers

Half hidden in the straw, the others were as silent and almost as still. Since they had been dropped upon the stone floor they had not moved, but lay in twisted, unnatural attitudes. Only their eyes showed that they lived. These were turned beseechingly upon the French Red Cross doctors, kneeling waist high in straw and unreeling long white bandages. The wounded watched them drawing slowly nearer, fighting off death until they came, clinging to life as shipwrecked sailors cling to a raft and watch boats pulling toward them.

A young German officer, his smart cavalry cloak torn and slashed and filthy with dried mud and blood, and with his eyes in bandages groped toward the pail of water, feeling his way with his boot, his arms stretched out clutching the air. To guide him a priest took his arm, and the officer turned and stumbled against him. Thinking the priest was one of his own men, he swore at him, and then to learn if he wore shoulder straps ran his fingers over the priest's shoulders, and, finding a silk cassock, said quickly in French: "Pardon me, my father, I am blind."

The archbishop of Rheims was at Rome electing a new Pope, and in his absence the young curé resident with the white hair was in charge. As he guided me through the wrecked cathedral his indignation and his fear of being unjust waged a fine battle, "Every summer," he said, "thousands of your fellow countrymen visit the cathedral. They come again and again. They love these beautiful windows. They will not permit them to be destroyed. Will you tell them what you saw?"

Wreckage in the Cathedral

It is no pleasure to tell what I saw. Shells had torn out some of the windows, the entire sash, glass and stone frame— all was gone; only a jagged hole was left. On the floor lay broken carvings, pieces of stone from flying buttresses outside that had been hurled through the embrasures, tangled masses of leaden window sashes, like twisted coils of barbed wire, and great brass candelabra. The steel ropes that supported them had been shot away, and they had plunged to the flagging below, carrying with them their scarlet silk tassels, heavy with the dust of centuries. And everywhere was broken glass. Not one of the famous windows was intact. None had been totally destroyed, but each had been shattered, and through the apertures the sun blazed blatantly.

We walked upon glass more precious than precious stones. It was beyond price. No one can replace it. Seven hundred years ago the secret of the glass died. Diamonds can be bought anywhere, pearls can be matched, but not the stained glass of Rheims. And under our feet, with straw and caked blood, it lay crushed into tiny fragments. When you held a piece of it between your eye and the sun it glowed with a light that never was on land or sea.

War is only waste. The German emperor thinks it is thousands of men in flashing breastplates at maneuvers, galloping past him, shouting "Hoch der Kaiser!" That is all of war that he has ever seen. I have seen a lot of it, and real war is his highborn officer with his eyes shot out, his peasant soldiers with their toes sticking stiffly through the straw, and the windows of Rheims, that for centuries with their beauty have glorified the Lord, swept into a dust heap.

Outside the Cathedral I found the bombardment of the city was still going forward with spirit and that the French batteries to the north and east were answering gun for gun. How people will act under unusual conditions no one can guess. Many of the citizens of Rheims were abandoning their homes and running through the streets leading west, trembling, weeping, incoherent with terror, carrying nothing with them. Others were continuing the routine of life with anxious, nervous faces, but making no other sign. The great majority had moved to the west of the city to the Paris gate and lined the road for miles, but had taken little or nothing with them, apparently intending to return at nightfall. They were all of the poorer class. The houses of the rich were closed, as were all the shops, except a few cafes and those that offered for sale bread, meat and medicine.

During yesterday morning the bombardment destroyed many houses. One to each block was the average, except around the cathedral, where two hotels that face it and the Palace of Justice had been pounded but not destroyed. Other shops and residences facing the cathedral had been ripped open from roof to cellar. In one a fire was burning briskly, and firemen were playing on it with hose. I was their only audience. A sight that at other times would have collected half of Rheims and blocked traffic in the excitement of the bombardment failed to attract. The Germans were using howitzers. Where shells hit in the street they tore up the Belgian blocks for a radius of five yards and made a hole as though a water main had burst. When they hit a house, that house had to be rebuilt. Before they struck it was possible to follow the direction of the shells by sound. It was like the jangling of many telegraph wires.

Effects of Bombardment

A hundred yards north of the cathedral I saw a house hit at the third story. The roof was of gray slate, high and sloping, with tall chimneys. When the shell exploded the roof and chimneys disappeared. You did not see them sink and tumble; they merely vanished. They had been a part of the skyline of Rheims; then a shell removed them and another roof fifteen feet lower down became the skyline.

I walked to the edge of the city, to the northeast, but at the outskirts all the streets were barricaded with carts and paving stones, and when I wanted to pass forward to the French batteries the officers in charge of the barricades refused permission. At this end of the town, held in reserve in case of a German advance, the streets were packed with infantry. The men were going from shop to shop trying to find one the Germans had not emptied. Tobacco was what they sought.

They told me they had been all the way to Belgium and back, but I never have seen them more fit. Where Germans are haggard and show need of food and sleep, the French were hard and moved quickly and were smiling.

One reason for this is that even if the commissariat is slow they are fed by their own people, and when in Belgium by the Allies. But when the Germans pass the people hide everything eatable, and bolt the doors and windows. And so when the German supply wagons fail to come up the men starve.

I went in search of the American Consul, William Bardel. Everybody seemed to know him and all men spoke well of him. They loved him because he stuck to his post, but the Mayor had sent for him and I could find neither him nor the Mayor.

When I left the Cathedral I had told my chauffeur to wait near it, not believing the Germans would continue to make it their point of attack. He waited until two houses within a hundred yards of him were knocked down, and then went away from there leaving word with the sentry that I could find him outside the gate to Paris. When I found him, he was well outside and refused to return, saying he would sleep in his car.

The Knitting Women

On the way back I met a steady stream of women and old men fleeing before the shells. Their state was very pitiful. Some of them seemed quite dazed with fear and ran dodging from one sidewalk to the other, and as shells burst over the city prayed aloud and crossed themselves. Others were busy behind the counters of their shops serving customers, and others stood in doorways holding in their hands their knitting. Frenchwomen of a certain class always knit. If they were waiting to be electrocuted they would continue knitting.

The bombardment had grown sharper and the rumble of guns was uninterrupted, growling like thunder after a summer storm, or shrieking as the shells passed to burst with jarring detonations. Under foot the pavements were inch deep with falling glass, and as you walked it tinkled musically. With inborn sense of order some of the housewives abandoned their knitting and calmly swept up the glass into neat piles. Habit is often so much stronger than fear. So is curiosity. All the boys and many young men and maidens were in the middle of the street watching to see where the shells struck and on the lookout for aeroplanes. When, about 5 o'clock, one sailed over the city, no one knew whether it was German or French, but everyone followed it, apparently intending if it dropped a bomb to be in at the death.

I found all the hotels closed, and on their doors I pounded in vain, and was planning to go back to my car when I was directed to the Hotel du Nord. It was open, and the proprietress, who was knitting, told me the teable d'hote dinner was ready. Not wishing to miss dinner, I halted an aged citizen who was fleeing from the city and asked him to carry a note to the American consul, inviting him to dinner. But the aged man said the consulate was close to the cathedral, and that to approach it was as much as his life was worth. I asked him how much his life was worth in money, and he said two francs.

He did not find the consul, and I shared the *table d'hote* with three tearful old French ladies, each of whom had husband or son at the front. That would seem to have been enough, without being shelled at home. It is a commonplace, but it is nevertheless true, that in war it is the women who suffer. The proprietress walked around the table, still knitting, and told us tales of German officers who, until the day before, had occupied her hotel, and her anecdotes were not intended to make German officers popular. Being at Rheims, I felt confident I would be served with the best champagne in existence, but it was quite the worst. And so another horror was added to war.

The bombardment ceased at 8 o'clock, but at 4 this morning it woke me, and as I departed for Paris salvos of French artillery were returning the German fire.

Before leaving I revisited the cathedral to see if during the night it had been further mutilated. Shells were still falling around it, and the square in front was deserted. In the falling rain the roofless houses, shattered windows and broken carvings that littered the street presented a picture of melancholy and useless desolation. Around three sides of the square not a building was intact. But facing the wreckage the bronze statue of Joan of Arc sat on her bronze charger, uninjured and untouched. In her right hand, lifted high above her, as though defying the German shells, someone overnight had lashed the flag of France.

New York Tribune
September 26, 1914

Rheims Cathedral Not Used by Army

Richard Harding Davis Says There Is No Ground for Only Conceivable Excuse of Germans for Shelling Distinguished Edifice

Rheims (via London), Sept. 24.—There is always the weaker brother who says "There are two sides to every question." To satisfy him concerning the destruction of the cathedral here I will first give what probably will be the German apology. Only one is conceivable That is that both towers of the cathedral were used by the French army as points of observation.

They were not. Both the French and German staffs mutually agreed that on the towers of the cathedral no quick-firing guns should be placed, and by both sides this agreement was observed. To protect innocent citizens against bombs dropped by German airships for two nights a searchlight was used in the towers, but feeling that this might be considered as a breach of the agreement as to mitrailleuse the searchlight was withdrawn.

Five days later, during which time the towers were not occupied and the cathedral had been converted into a hospital for German wounded and Red Cross flags were hanging from both towers, the Germans opened fire upon it. This afternoon, two days later, when the Abbe Chinot and I spent three hours in what is left of the cathedral, they still were shelling it. Two shells fell within twenty-five yards of us.

The indignation of the world at this latest atrocity reached the Berlin Foreign Office this morning. That the bombardment could continue shows the value the German army places on the opinion of the civilized world.

For some months the northeast tower of the cathedral has been under repair and surrounded by scaffolding. On Saturday afternoon a shell set fire to the roof of the cathedral. The fire spread to the scaffolding and from the scaffolding to the wooden frames of the portals, some hundreds of years old.

Father Chinot, abbe of the chapel of the cathedral, young, alert and daring, ran out upon the scaffolding and tried to cut the cords that bound it. In other parts of the city the Fire Department was engaged with fires lit by the bombardment and, unaided, the flames gained on them. Seeing this, he called for volunteers, and under direction of Archbishop Landreaux of Rheims, the wounded Germans were carried on stretchers from the burning building. The rescuing parties were not a minute too soon. Already, from the roofs, molten lead, as deadly as bullets, was falling among the wounded, and the blazing doors had turned the straw on which they lay into a prairie fire. Splashed by the lead and threatened by the falling timbers the priests, at risk of life and limb, carried out all but one of the wounded Germans, sixty in all. But after bearing them to safety the charges were confronted with a new danger. Inflamed by the sight of their own dead (four hundred citizens having been killed by the bombardment) and by the loss of their cathedral the people of Rheims, who were gathered about the burning building, called for the lives of the German prisoners.

"They are barbarians," they cried. "Kill them!"

Archbishop Landreux and the Abbe Chinot placed themselves in front of the wounded.

"Before you kill them," they cried, "you must first kill us!"

This is not highly colored action, but fact. It is more than fact. It is victory, for the picture of the venerable Archbishop, with his cathedral blazing behind him, facing a mob of his own people in defense of their enemies, will always live in the annals of this war and of the Catholic Church.

There were other features of this fire and bombardment of which the Catholic Church will not fail to take advantage.

Leaden roofs were destroyed, oak timbers that for several hundred years had supported them were destroyed, stone statues and flying buttresses weighing many tons were smashed into powder, but in all the chapels not a single crucifix was touched, not one waxen or wooden image of the Virgin disturbed, not one painting of the Holy Family marred.

You could explain it to suit yourself as a coincidence or miracle, but the fact remains.

I saw the Gobelin tapestries, more precious than spun gold, intact, while sparks tell about them, and lying beneath them iron bolts twisted by fire, broken roof trees, shattered carvings, and beams that were still smoldering.

But the special providence that saved the altars was not omnipotent. Windows that were the glory of the cathedral were wrecked. Through some the shells had passed. Others the explosions had blown into tiny fragments. When on Friday I saw in the stained glass gaping holes this afternoon the whole window had been torn from the wall. Statues of saints and crusaders and angels and cherubim lay in mingled fragments. The great bells, each as large as the Liberty Bell, in Philadelphia, that for hundreds of years for Rheims have sounded the Angelus were torn from their oak girders and melted into black masses of silver and copper without shape and without sound.

Never have I looked upon a picture of such pathos, of such wanton and wicked destruction! The towers still stand. The walls still stand, for beneath the roofs of lead the roof of stone remained, but what is intact is a pitiful, distorted mass where once were exquisite and noble features. It is like the face of a beautiful saint scarred with vitriol.

It was not only carved stone and stained glass that the Germans wiped out, but the traditions of seven hundred years. A few days ago when one walked through the cathedral the scene was set as it was when kings were crowned in these same surroundings. You stood where Joan of Arc received the homage of France. Today you walk on charred ashes, broken stone and shattered glass. Where once the light was dim and holy now through great breaches in the walls rain splashes. The spirit of the place has gone. By Huns and Vandals it has been ravaged and desecrated.

Outside the cathedral, in the direction from which the shells came, for two city blocks every house is destroyed. The palace of the Archbishop is in ruins. His chapel and the robbing room of the kings are cellars filled with rubble. Of them only crumbling walls remain, and on the south and west facades of the cathedral the flying buttresses and the statues of kings, angels and saints are mangled and shapeless.

When darkness came Monday night, when I was there, the bombardment paused. It ended with a few shells that struck within twenty-five yards of the cathedral. So it would appear that with their work the German wrecking crew are not yet satisfied. The French guns that are answering may have what is left of the cathedral, but meanwhile public opinion in America, if trained on Germany, would be equally effective.

Judging by cable messages which I have received, objecting to what I told of what I saw at Louvain, the German vote at home must be large and someone must want it. But there must also be those who honor this Church that nursed them.

If her temples, her works of art, her historic shrines are not to go the way of Louvain and Rheims they should now protest. Is there not also an Irish vote?

New York Tribune
September 29, 1914

Rheims a Wreck Around Cathedral

Davis Describes Heartrending Devastation and Says That if Kaiser's Excuse Is True, He Should Court Martial His Artillery Officers for Bad Marksmanship

Paris, Sept. 25 (Delayed in transmission).—This morning in the Paris papers the official German excuse for the bombardment of Rheims was published. It stated that the French batteries were so placed that in replying to them it was impossible to avoid shelling the city.

It would not be proper for me to tell where the French batteries were, but I know exactly where they were, and if the German guns aimed at them by error, missed them and hit the cathedral the German marksmanship is deteriorating. To find the range the artillery sends what in the American army are called brace shots—one aimed at a point beyond the mark and one short of it. From the explosions of these two shells the gunner is able to determine how far he is off the target, and accordingly regulates his sights. Not more, at the most, than three of these experimental brace shots should be necessary, and as one of each brace is purposely aimed to fall short of the target only three German shells, or, as there were two French positions, six German shells should have fallen beyond the batteries and into the city. And yet for four days the city was bombarded.

To make sure, I today asked French, English and American army officers what margin of error they thought excusable after the range was determined. They all agreed that after his range was found an artillery officer who missed it by from fifty to one hundred yards ought to be court-martialed. The Germans "missed" by one mile.

I walked over the district that had been destroyed by these accidental shots, and it stretched from the northeastern outskirts of Rheims in a straight line to the cathedral. Shells that fell short of the cathedral for a quarter of a mile destroyed entirely three city blocks. The heart of this district is the Place Godinot. In every direction at a distance of a mile from the Place Godinot I passed houses wrecked by shells—south at the Paris gate, north at the railroad station.

Aim at City, Then May Hit Battery

There is no part of Rheims that these shells aimed at French batteries did not hit. If Rheims accepts the German excuse she might suggest to them that the next time they bombard, if they aim at the city they may hit the French batteries.

The Germans claim that the damage done was from fires, not shells. But that is not the case; destruction by fire was slight. Houses wrecked by shells where there was no fire outnumber those that were burning ten to one. In no house was there probably any other fire than that in the kitchen stove, and that had been smothered by falling masonry and tiles.

Except for Red Cross volunteers seeking among the ruins for wounded, I found that part of the city that had suffered completely deserted. Shells still were falling, and houses as yet intact and those partly destroyed were empty. You saw pitiful attempts to save the pieces. In places, as though evictions were going forward, chairs, pictures, cooking pans, bedding were piled in heaps. There was none to guard them; certainly there was no one so unfeeling as to disturb them.

I saw neither looting nor any effort to guard against it. In their common danger and horror the citizens of Rheims of all classes seemed drawn closely together. The manner of all was subdued and gentle, like those who stand at an open grave.

The shells played the most inconceivable pranks. In some streets the houses and shops along one side were entirely wiped out, and on the other untouched. In the Rue du Cardinal de Lorraine every house was gone. Where they once stood were cellars, filled with powdered stone. Tall chimneys that one would have thought a strong wind might dislodge were holding themselves erect, while the surrounding walls, three feet thick, had been crumpled into rubbish.

In some houses a shell had removed one room only, and as neatly as though it were the work of masons and carpenters. It was as though the shell had a grievance against the lodger in that particular room. The waste was appalling.

Child's Doll Lies Smiling Amid Ruins

Among the ruins I saw a good painting in rags and in gardens statues covered with the moss of centuries smashed. In many places, still on the pedestal, you would see a headless Venus or a flying Mercury chopped off at his waist.

Long streamers of ivy, that during a century had crept higher and higher up the wall of some noble mansion until they were part of it, and clung to it, although it was divided into a thousand fragments. Of one house all that was left standing was a slice of the front wall just wide enough to bear a sign reading "This house is for sale; elegantly furnished." Nothing else of that house remained.

In some streets of the destroyed area I met not one living person. The noise made by my feet kicking the broken glass was the only sound. The silence, the gaping holes in the sidewalk, the ghastly tributes to the power of the shells, and the complete desolation, made more desolate by the bright sunshine, gave you a curious feeling that the end of the world had come and you were the only survivor.

The impression was aided by the sight of many rare and valuable articles with no one guarding them. They were things of price that one may not carry into the next world, but which in this are kept under lock and key.

In the Rue de l'Universite at my leisure I could have ransacked shop after shop, or from the shattered drawing rooms filled my pockets. Shopkeepers had gone without waiting to lock their doors, and in houses the fronts of which were down you could see that, in order to save their lives, the inmates had fled at a moment's warning.

Bursting Shells' Fantastic Trick

In another house everything was destroyed except the marble mantelpiece over the fireplace in the drawing room. On this stood a terra cotta statuette of Harlequin. It is one you have often seen. The legs are wide apart, the arms folded, the head thrown back in an ecstasy of laughter. It looked exactly as though it were laughing at the wreckage with which it was surrounded. No one could have placed it where it was after the house fell, for the approach to it was still on fire. Of all the fantastic tricks played by the bursting shells it was the most curious.

Outside the wrecked area were many shops belonging to American firms, but each of them had escaped injury. They were filled with American typewriters, sewing machines and cameras. A number of cafes bearing the sign "American bar" testified to the nationality and tastes of many tourists.

I found our consul, William Barder, at the consulate. He is a fine type of the German-American citizen and, since the war began, with his wife and son has held the fort and tactfully looked after the interests of both Americans and Germans. On both sides of him shells had damaged the houses immediately adjoining. The one across the street had been destroyed and two neighbors killed.

The street in front of the consulate is a mass of fallen stone, and the morning I called on Mr. Bardel a shell had hit his neighbor's chestnut tree, filled his garden with chestnut burrs and blown out the glass of his windows. He was patching the holes with brown wrapping paper, but was chiefly concerned because in his own garden the dahlias were broken. During the first part of the bombardment, when firing became too hot for him, he had retreated with his family to the corner of the street, where are the cellars of the Roderers, the champagne people.

There are worse places in which to hide in than a champagne cellar, and I hope Secretary Bryan will not hold it against him. He had no choice. In Rheims the grape juice cellars are very few—of Mr. Bryan's sort.

Mr. Bardel has lived six years in Rheims and estimates the damage done to property by shells at $30,000,000, and says that unless the seat of military operations is removed the champagne crop for this year will be entirely wasted. It promised to be an especially good year. The seasons were propitious, being dry when sun was needed and wet when rain was needed, but, unless the grapes are gathered this week, the crops will be lost.

Bad Outlook For Broadway

Of interest to Broadway is the fact that in Rheims, or rather in her cellars, are stored nearly fifty million bottles of champagne belonging to six of the best known houses. Should shells reach these bottles, the high price of living in the lobster palaces will be proportionately increased.

Mr. Bardel asked me to send his love to his son. H.T. Bardel, of 1635 New York Ave., Brooklyn, saying "We are all safe and well." I was delayed in sending this message because, outside of Rheims at a certain place, with my companions, Gerald Morgan, of "McClure's Magazine"; Ashmead Bartlett, of "The London Daily Telegraph," and Captain Granville Fortescue, I was arrested.

Under escort we were taken to Paris. Once there, every courtesy was shown us. We were detained only one night at the headquarters of the General Staff. The following morning, Mr. Herrick, our ambassador, acting through our military attaché, Colonel Spencer Cosby, arranged that we should be set at liberty on our giving our word that for eight days we would not leave Paris or in any way communicate with anyone concerning what movements of the Allies we might have seen.

As the destruction of Rheims does not come in that category, I have concluded the account of my visit to that unhappy city at the point where the gendarmes so abruptly interrupted it.

The story of our arrest my companions can tell. This year I have been so frequently in jail that you readers must be as weary of it as I am. Then, again, perhaps I flatter myself. In any case, I would be ungrateful if I did not acknowledge the prompt assistance of Mr. Herrick and Colonel Cosby and the courtesy of the French officers of the General Staff. We were less prisoners than their guests, and should I be invited to spend another weekend in Cherche Midi-Prison, I would accept with pleasure.

But I have a feeling that next time I am arrested it will not be in Europe for trying to see this war, but in Westchester County for overspeeding. I have investigated enough European jails. At home there must be some equally bad. One should see America first.

New York Tribune
October 3, 1914

French Capital Sees Its Oldtime Activity

Richard Harding Davis Tells of Remarkable Change in Three Weeks—Cafes and Stores Reopen and Boulevards Are Again Crowded

Paris is herself again, or nearly so. Those who were suddenly called away on business to Bordeaux or London are back. By a fortunate coincidence each of them was able to wind up his affairs and return the day after the Germans were pushed across the Aisne.

Three weeks ago, when I first arrived here, Paris was as desolate as Philadelphia on a rainy Sunday, but today the boulevards are as crowded as the Atlantic City boardwalk in July. This is true not only in the show places, but over all the city. Yesterday I walked to the American Hospital at Neuilly, and the cafes on both sides of the Avenue de la Grande Armee were crowded and every shop was open.

On Sunday it was impossible to guess where all the people who blocked the boulevards came from and where they had been hidden. When the Germans were within twenty miles of Paris the people you saw on the boulevards you could count on both hands, and half of them were German. But on Sunday they overflowed from the sidewalks into the street; whole families were promenading, old people, young people, all in their best clothes. Where they have been keeping themselves is a mystery. We have seen no signs of the returning prodigals, no cabs piled high with luggage, no porters bringing hand baggage. As suddenly as they vanished, as suddenly have they reappeared.

With customers returning and no Germans to fear, the shops along the Rue de la Paix are beginning to open and, as in spring, each morning a new flower greets you, so now in that famous thoroughfare where were bleak iron shutters, every morning another shop opens its portals and the window blooms with robes, manteaux or diamond tiaras. To help competition they came none too soon. For weeks we have had to buy all our diamond tiaras at one shop.

Children Were Greatly Missed

The thing you missed perhaps most were the children in the Avenue des Champs Elysees. For generations over that part of the public garden the children have held sway. They knew it belonged to them, and into the gravel walks drove their tin spades with the same sense of ownership as at Deauville they dig up the shore. Their straw hats and bare legs, their Normandy nurses, with enormous headdresses, blue for a boy and pink for a girl, were one of the most familiar sights of Paris. And when they vanished they left a dreary wilderness. You could look for a mile from the Place de la Concorde to the Arc de Triomphe and not see a child. The stalls where they bought hoops and skipping ropes, the flying wooden horses, Punch and Judy shows, booths where with milk they refreshed themselves and with bonbons made themselves ill, all were deserted and boarded up, as desolate as the summer resort in February. But four days ago the children, nurses and baby carriages came back, Punch and Judy shows reopened, and flying horses are pursuing each other in that hopeless race that is never decided.

The closing down of the majority of the shops and hotels was not due to a desire on the part of those employed in them to avoid the Germans, but to get at the Germans. On shop after shop are signs reading "The proprietor and staff are with the colors," or "The personnel of the establishment is mobilized," or "Monsieur — informs his clients that he is with his regiment."

In the absence of men at the front French women, at all times capable and excellent managers, have surpassed themselves. In my hotel there are employed seven women and one man. In another hotel I visited the entire staff was composed of women.

American Banker's Offer Refused

An American banker here offered his twenty-two polo ponies to the government. They were refused as not heavy enough. He did not know that, and supposed he had lost them. He learned yesterday from the wife of his trainer, a French woman, that those employed in his stables at Versailles who had not gone to the front at the approach of the Germans had fled and that for three weeks his string of twenty-two horses had been fed, groomed and exercised by the trainer's wife and her two little girls.

To an American it is very gratifying to hear the praise of the French and English for the American ambulance at Neuilly. It is the outgrowth of the American hospital, and at the start of this war was organized by Mrs. Herrick, wife of our ambassador, and other ladies of the American colony in Paris and the American doctors. They took over the Lycee Pasteur, an enormous school at Neuilly, that had just been finished and never occupied, and converted it into what is a most splendidly equipped hospital. In walking over the building you find it hard to believe that it was intended for any other than its present use. The operating rooms, kitchens, wards, rooms for operating by Roentgen rays, and even a chapel have been installed.

The organization and system are of the highest order. Everyone in it is American. The doctors are the best in Paris. The nurses and orderlies are both especially trained for the work and volunteers. The spirit of helpfulness and unselfishness is everywhere apparent. Certain members of the American colony, who never in their lives thought of anyone save themselves and of how to escape boredom, are toiling like chambermaids and hall porters, perfecting most disagreeable tasks, not for a few hours a week, but unceasingly, day after day. No task is too heavy for them or too squalid. They are for all alike—Germans, English, major generals and black Turcos.

Staff of Hospital Comprises 150

There are three hundred patients. The staff of the hospital numbers 150. It is composed of the best known American doctors in Paris and a few from New York. Among the volunteer nurses and attendants are wives of bankers here, American girls who have married French titles, and girls who since the war came have lost employment as teachers of languages, stenographers and governesses. The men are members of the Jockey Club, art students, medical students, clerks and boulevardiers. They are all working together in most admirable harmony and under an organization that in its efficiency far surpasses that of any other hospital in Paris. Later it is going to split the American colony in twain. If you did not work in the American ambulance you won't belong.

Attached to the hospital is a squadron of automobile ambulances, ten of which were presented by the Ford Company and ten purchased. Their chassis have been covered with khaki hoods and fitted to carry two wounded men and attendants. On their runs they are accompanied by automobiles with medical supplies, tires and gasoline. The ambulances scout at the rear of the battle line and carry back those which the field hospitals cannot handle.

The other day I watched orderlies who accompany these ambulances handling about forty English wounded, transferring them from the automobiles to the reception hall, and the smartness and intelligence with which the members of each crew worked together was like that of a champion polo team. The editor of a London paper, who is in Paris investigating English hospital conditions, witnessed the same performance and told me that in handling the wounded it surpassed in efficiency anything he ever had seen.

First Thought Was of Mother

We have had another visit from a gallant general—a German. Hidden by clouds, he dropped five bombs into Paris while everybody either was at church or was going to church and succeeded in killing a lawyer and in tearing the leg off of a little girl. When the gendarme picked her up she said, "Don't tell my mother how serious it is." Our Ambassador Herrick, with Hugh Frazier, second secretary of the embassy, passed over the place where the bomb fell just a few minutes before it struck. I visited the place where a bomb fell in the Avenue du Trocadero and it was difficult to see how anyone within a radius of fifty yards survived. Every housetop and window within that circle was hit, and gravel stones from the street were driven several inches into trunks of trees.

It may be that these German aviators are reluctantly carrying out orders, but as daredevils they are rapidly losing caste. In comparison with them the sharpshooter and the spy become heroic figures. The brain of a man who, out of rifle range and hidden by clouds, drops bombs among people occupied in nothing more hostile than in going to church would be worth dissecting. It is a performance as free from danger and requiring only the same kind of courage as that which leads a small boy to throw stones at the Empire State Express when it passes him at seventy miles an hour.

Scribner's
November, 1914

The Germans in Brussels

WHEN, on August 4, the *Lusitania*, with lights doused and air-ports sealed, slipped out of New York harbor the crime of the century was only a few days old. And for three days those on board the *Lusitania* of the march of the great events were ignorant. Whether or no between England and Germany the struggle for the supremacy of the sea had begun we could not learn.

But when, on the third day, we came on deck the news was written against the sky. Swinging from the funnels, sailors were painting out the scarlet-and-black colors of the Cunard line and substituting a mouse-like gray. Overnight we had passed into the hands of the admiralty, and the Lusitania had emerged a cruiser. That to possible German warships she might not disclose her position, she sent no wireless messages. But she could receive them; and at breakfast in the ship's newspaper appeared those she had overnight snatched from the air. Among them, without a Scarehead, in the most modest of type, we read: "England and Germany have declared war." Seldom has news so momentous been conveyed so simply, or, by the Englishmen on board, more calmly accepted. For any exhibition they gave of excitement or concern, the news the radio brought them might have been the result of a by-election.

Later in the morning they gave us another exhibition of that repression of feeling, of that disdain of hysteria, that is a national characteristic, and is what Mr. Kipling meant when he wrote: "But oh, beware my country, when my country grows polite!"

Word came that in the North Sea the English warships had destroyed the German fleet. To celebrate this battle which, were the news authentic, would rank with Trafalgar and might mean the end of the war, one of the ship's officers exploded a detonating bomb. Nothing else exploded. Whatever feelings of satisfaction our English cousins experienced they concealed.

Under like circumstances, on an American ship, we would have tied down the siren, sung the doxology, and broken everything on the bar. As it was, the Americans instinctively flocked to the smoking-room and drank to the British navy. While this ceremony was going forward, from the promenade deck we heard tumultuous shouts and cheers. We believed that, relieved of our presence, our English friends had given way to rejoicings. But when we went on deck we found them deeply engaged in cricket. The cheers we had heard were over the retirement of a batsman who had just been given out, leg before wicket.

When we reached London we found no idle boasting, no vainglorious jingoism. The war that Germany had forced upon them the English accepted with a grim determination to see it through and, while they were about it, to make it final. They were going ahead with no false illusions. Fully did every one appreciate the enormous task, the personal loss that lay before him. But each, in his or her way, went into the fight determined to do his duty. There was no dismay, no hysteria, no "mafficking."

The secrecy maintained by the press and the people regarding anything concerning the war, the knowledge of which might embarrass the War Office, was one of the most admirable and remarkable conspiracies of silence that modern times have known. Officers of the same regiment even with each other would not discuss the orders they had received. In no single newspaper, with no matter how lurid a past record for sensationalism, was there a line to suggest that a British army had landed in France and that Great Britain was at war. Sooner than embarrass those who were conducting the fight, the individual English man and woman in silence suffered the most cruel anxiety of mind. Of that, on my return to London from Brussels, I was given an illustration. I had written to the

Daily Chronicle telling where in Belgium I had seen a wrecked British air-ship, and beside it the grave of the aviator. I gave the information in order that the family of the dead officer might find the grave and bring the body home. The morning the letter was published an elderly gentleman, a retired officer of the navy, called at my rooms. His son, he said, was an aviator, and for a month of him no word had come. His mother was distressed. Could I describe the air-ship I had seen?

I was not keen to play the messenger of ill tidings, so I tried to gain time.

"What make of aeroplane does your son drive?" I asked.

As though preparing for a blow, the old gentleman drew himself up, and looked me steadily in the eyes.

"A Bleriot monoplane," he said.

I was as relieved as though his boy were one of my own kinsmen.

"The air-ship I saw," I told him, "was an Avro biplane!"

Of the two I appeared much the more pleased.

The retired officer bowed.

"I thank you," he said. "It will be good news for his mother."

"But why didn't you go to the War Office?" I asked.

He reproved me firmly.

"They have asked us not to question them," he said, "and when they are working for all I have no right to embarrass them with my personal trouble."

As the chance of obtaining credentials with the British army appeared doubtful, I did not remain in London, but at once crossed to Belgium.

Before the Germans came, Brussels was an imitation Paris—especially along the inner boulevards she was Paris at her best. And her great parks, her lakes gay with pleasure-boats or choked with lilypads, her haunted forests, where your taxicab would startle the wild deer, are the most beautiful I have ever seen in any city in the world. As in the days of the

Second Empire, Louis Napoleon bedecked Paris, so Leopold decorated Brussels. In her honor and to his own glory he gave her new parks, filled in her moats along her ancient fortifications, laid out boulevards shaded with trees, erected arches, monuments, museums. That these jewels he hung upon her neck were wrung from the slaves of the Congo does not make them the less beautiful. And before the Germans came, the life of the people of Brussels was in keeping with the elegance, beauty, and joyousness of their surroundings.

At the Palace Hotel, which is the clearing-house for the social life of Brussels, we found everybody taking his ease at a little iron table on the sidewalk. It was night, but the city was as light as noonday— brilliant, elated, full of movement and color. For Liege was still held by the Belgians, and they believed that all along the line they were holding back the German army. It was no wonder they were jubilant. They had a right to be proud. They had been making history. In order to give them time to mobilize, the Allies had asked them for two days to delay the German invader. They had held him back for fifteen. As David went against Goliath, they had repulsed the German. And as yet there had been no reprisals, no destruction of cities, no murdering of noncombatants; war still was something glad and glorious.

The signs of it were the Boy Scouts, everywhere helping everyone, carrying messages, guiding strangers, directing traffic; and Red Cross nurses and aviators from England, smart Belgian officers exclaiming bitterly over the delay in sending them forward, and private automobiles upon the enameled sides of which the transport officer with a piece of chalk had scratched, "For His Majesty," and piled the silk cushions high with ammunition. From table to table young girls passed jangling tiny tin milk-cans. They were supplicants, begging money for the wounded. There were so many of them and so often they made their rounds that, to protect you from themselves, if you subscribed a lump sum, you were exempt and were given a badge to prove you were immune.

Except for these signs of the times you would not have known Belgium was at war. The spirit of the people was undaunted. Into their daily lives the conflict had penetrated only like a burst of martial music. Rather than depressing, it inspired them. Wherever you ventured, you found them undismayed. And in those weeks during which events moved so swiftly that now they seem months in the past, we were as free as in our own "home town" to go where we chose.

For the war correspondent those were the happy days! Like everyone else, from the proudest nobleman to the boy in wooden shoes, we were given a laisser-passer, which gave us permission to go anywhere; this with a passport was our only credential. Proper credentials to accompany the army in the field had been formerly refused me by the war officers of England, France, and Belgium. So in Brussels each morning I chartered an automobile and without credentials joined the first army that happened to be passing. Sometimes you stumbled upon an escarmouche, sometimes you fled from one, sometimes you drew blank. Over our early coffee we would study the morning papers and, as in the glad days of racing at home, from them try to dope out the winners. If we followed *La Derniere Heure* we would go to Namur; *L'Etoile* was strong for Tirlemont. Would we lose if we plunged on Wavre? Again, the favorite seemed to be Louvain. On a straight tip from the legation the English correspondents were going to motor to Diest. From a Belgian officer we had been given inside information that the fight would be pulled off at Gembloux. And, unencumbered by even a sandwich, and too wise to carry a field-glass or a camera, each would depart upon his separate errand, at night returning to a perfectly served dinner and a luxurious bed. For the news-gatherers it was a game of chance. The wisest veterans would cast their nets south and see only harvesters in the fields, the amateurs would lose their way to the north and find themselves facing an army corps or running a gauntlet of shell-fire. It was like throwing a handful of coins on the table hoping that one might rest upon the winning number. Over the map of Belgium we threw ourselves. Some days we landed on the right color, on others we saw no more than we would see at state maneuvers.

Judging by his questions, the lay brother seems to think that the chief trouble of the war correspondent is dodging bullets. It is not. It consists in trying to bribe a station-master to carry you on a troop train, or in finding forage for your horse. What wars I have seen have taken place in spots isolated and inaccessible, far from the haunts of men. By day you followed the fight and tried to find the censor, and at night you sat on a cracker-box and by the light of a candle struggled to keep awake and to write deathless prose. In Belgium it was not like that. The automobile which Gerald Morgan, of the London *Daily Telegraph*, and I shared was of surpassing beauty, speed, and comfort. It was as long as a Plant freight-car and as yellow; and from it flapped in the breeze more English, Belgian, French, and Russian flags than fly from the roof of the New York Hippodrome. Whenever we sighted an army we lashed the flags of its country to our headlights, and at sixty miles an hour bore down upon it. The army always first arrested us, and then, on learning our nationality, asked if it were true that America had joined the Allies. After I had punched his ribs a sufficient number of times Morgan learned to reply without winking that it had.

In those days the sun shone continuously; the roads, except where we ran on the blocks that made Belgium famous, were perfect; and overhead for miles noble trees met and embraced. The country was smiling and beautiful. In the fields the women (for the men were at the front) were gathering the crops, the stacks of golden grain stretched from village to village. The houses in these were whitewashed and, the better to advertise chocolates, liqueurs, and automobile tires, were painted a cobalt blue; their roofs were of red tiles, and they sat in gardens of purple cabbages or gaudy hollyhocks. In the orchards the pear-trees were bent with fruit.

We never lacked for food; always, when we lost the trail and "checked," or burst a tire, there was an inn with fruit trees trained to lie flat against the wall, or to spread over arbors and trellises. Beneath these, close by the roadside, we sat and drank red wine, and devoured omelets and vast slabs of rye bread. At night we raced back to the city, through twelve miles of parks, to enameled bath-tubs, shaded electric light, and iced champagne; while before our table passed all the night life of a great city. And for suffering these hardships of war our papers paid us large sums.

On such a night as this, the night of August 18, strange folk in wooden shoes and carrying bundles, and who looked like emigrants from Ellis Island, appeared in front of the restaurant. Instantly they were swallowed up in a crowd and the dinner parties, napkins in hand, flocked into the Place Rogier and increased the throng around them.

"The Germans!" those in the heart of the crowd called over their shoulders. "The Germans are at Louvain!"

That afternoon I had conscientiously cabled my paper that there were no Germans anywhere near Louvain. I had been west of Louvain, and the particular column of the French army to which I had attached myself certainly saw no Germans.

"They say," whispered those nearest the fugitives, "the German shells are falling in Louvain. Ten houses are on fire!" Ten houses! How monstrous it sounded! Ten houses of innocent country folk destroyed. In those days such a catastrophe was unbelievable. We smiled knowingly.

"Refugees always talk like that," we said wisely. "The Germans would not bombard an unfortified town. And, besides, there are no Germans south of Liege."

The morning following in my room I heard from the Place Rogier the warnings of many motor horns. At great speed innumerable automobiles were approaching, all coming from the west through the Boulevard du Regent, and without slackening speed passing northeast toward Ghent, Bruges, and the coast. The number increased and the warnings became insistent. At eight o'clock they had sent out a sharp request for right of way; at nine in number they had trebled, and the note of the sirens was raucous, harsh, and peremptory. At ten no longer were there disconnected warnings, but from the horns and sirens issued one long, continuous scream. It was like the steady roar of a gale in the rigging, and it spoke in abject panic. The voices of the cars racing past were like the voices of human beings driven with fear. From the front of the hotel we watched them. There were taxicabs, racing-cars, limousines. They were crowded with women and children of the rich, and of the nobility and gentry from the great chateaux far to the west. Those who occupied them were white-faced with the dust of the road, with weariness and fear. In cars magnificently upholstered, padded, and cushioned were piled trunks, handbags, dressing-cases. The women had dressed at a moment's warning, as though at a cry of fire. Many had travelled throughout the night, and in their arms the children, snatched from the pillows, were sleeping.

But more appealing were the peasants. We walked out along the inner boulevards to meet them, and found the side streets blocked with their carts. Into these they had thrown mattresses, or bundles of grain, and heaped upon them were families of three generations. Old men in blue smocks, white-haired and bent, old women in caps, the daughters dressed in their one best frock and hat, and clasping in their hands all that was left to them, all that they could stuff into a pillow-case or flour-sack. The tears rolled down their brown, tanned faces. To the people of Brussels who crowded around them they spoke in hushed, broken phrases. The terror of what they had escaped or of what they had seen was upon them. They had harnessed the plough-horse to the dray or market-wagon and to the invaders had left everything. What, they asked, would befall the livestock they had abandoned, the ducks on the pond, the cattle in the field? Who would feed them and give them water? At the question the tears would break out afresh. Heartbroken, weary, hungry, they passed in an unending caravan. With them, all fleeing from the same foe, all moving in one direction, were family carriages, the servants on the box in disordered livery, as they had served dinner, or coatless, but still in the striped waistcoats and silver buttons of grooms or footmen, and bicyclers with bundles strapped to their shoulders, and men and women stumbling on foot, carrying their children. Above it all rose the breathless scream of the racing cars, as they rocked and skidded, with brakes grinding and mufflers open; with their own terror creating and spreading terror.

Though eager in sympathy, the people of Brussels themselves were undisturbed. Many still sat at the little iron tables and smiled pityingly upon the strange figures of the peasants. They had had their trouble for nothing, they said. It was a false alarm. There were no Germans nearer than Liege. And besides, should the Germans come, the civil guard would meet them.

But, better informed than they, that morning the American minister, Brand Whitlock, and the Marquis Villalobar, the Spanish minister, had called upon the burgomaster and advised him not to defend the city. As Whitlock pointed out, with the force at his command, which was the citizen soldiery, he could delay the entrance of the Germans by only an hour, and in that hour many innocent lives would be wasted, and monuments of great beauty, works of art that belong not alone to Brussels but to the world, would be destroyed. Burgomaster Max, who is a splendid and worthy representative of a long line of burgomasters, placing his hand upon his heart, said: "Honor requires it."

To show that in the protection of the Belgian government he had full confidence, Mr. Whitlock had not as yet shown his colors. But that morning when he left the Hotel de Ville he hung the American flag over his legation, and over that of the British. Those of us who had elected to remain in Brussels moved our belongings to a hotel across the street from the legation. Not taking any chances, for my own use I reserved a green-leather sofa in the legation itself.

Except that the cafés were empty of Belgian officers, and of English correspondents, whom, had they remained, the Germans would have arrested, there was not, up to late in the afternoon of the 19th of August, in the life and conduct of the citizens any perceptible change. They could not have shown a finer spirit. They did not know the city would not be defended; and yet before them on the morrow was the prospect of a battle which Burgomaster Max had announced would be contested to the very heart of the city, and as usual the cafés blazed like open fireplaces and the people sat at the little iron tables. Even when, like great buzzards, two German aeroplanes sailed slowly across Brussels, casting shadows of events to come, the people regarded them only with curiosity. The next morning the shops were open, the streets were crowded. But overnight the soldier-king had sent word that Brussels must not oppose the invaders; and at the gendarmerie the civil guard, reluctantly and protesting, some even in tears, turned in their rifles and uniforms.

The change came at ten in the morning. It was as though a wand had waved and from a fete day on the Continent we had been wafted to London on a rainy Sunday. The boulevards fell suddenly empty. There was not a house that was not closely shuttered. Along the route by which we now knew the Germans were advancing, it was as though the plague stalked. That no one should fire from a window, that to the conquerors no one should offer insult. Burgomaster Max sent out as special constables men he trusted. Their badge of authority was a walking-stick and a piece of paper fluttering from a buttonhole. These, the police, and the servants and caretakers of the houses that lined the boulevards alone were visible. At eleven o'clock, unobserved but by this official audience, down the Boulevard Waterloo came the advance-guard of the German army. It consisted of three men, a captain and two privates on bicycles. Their rifles were slung across their shoulders, they rode unwarily, with as little concern as the members of a touring-club out for a holiday. Behind them, so close upon each other that to cross from one sidewalk to the other was not possible, came the Uhlans, infantry, and the guns. For two hours I watched them, and then, bored with the monotony of it, returned to the hotel. After an hour, from beneath my window I still could hear them; another hour and another went by. They still were passing. Boredom gave way to wonder. The thing fascinated you, against your will, dragged you back to the sidewalk and held you there open-eyed. No longer was it regiments of men marching, but something uncanny, inhuman; a force of nature like a landslide, a tidal wave, or lava sweeping down a mountain. It was not of this earth, but mysterious, ghostlike. The uniform aided this impression. In it each man moved under a cloak of invisibility. To describe its gray-green color is impossible, because it has no color, and yet it absorbs all colors, and reflects no light. We saw it first in the warm summer sunshine, later under the glare of electric lamps, hours later in the gray of the morning. At all times the men clothed in it were indistinguishable. They blended with the gray stones of the street, with the green of the trees; they shifted and merged like drifting fog. Even as you pointed they dissolved into thin air. It was like a conjuring trick. It is a fact that often you would see advancing toward you a troop of horses and you could not see the men who rode them.

  All through the night, like the tumult of a river when it races between the cliffs of a canyon, in my sleep I could hear the steady roar of the passing army. And when early in the morning I went to the window the chain of steel was still unbroken. As a correspondent I have seen all the great armies and the military processions at the coronations, in Russia, England, and Spain, and our own inaugural parades down Pennsylvania Avenue, but those armies and processions were made up of men. This was a machine, endless, tireless, with the delicate organization of a watch and the brute power of a steamroller. And for three days and three nights through Brussels it roared and rumbled, a cataract of molten lead. The infantry marched singing, with their iron-shod boots beating out the time. In each regiment there were two thousand men and at the same instant, in perfect unison, two thousand iron brogans struck the granite street. It was like the blows from giant pile-drivers. The Uhlans followed, the hoofs of their magnificent horses ringing like thousands of steel hammers breaking stones in a road; and after them the giant siege-guns rumbling, growling, the mitrailleuse with drag-chains clanking, the field-pieces with creaking axles, complaining brakes, the grinding of the steel-rimmed wheels against the stones echoing and re-echoing from the house-front. When at night for an instant the machine halted, the silence awoke you, as at sea you wake when the screw stops. For three days and three nights the column of gray, with fifty thousand bayonets and fifty thousand lances, with gray transport wagons, gray ammunition-carts, gray ambulances, gray cannon, like a river of steel cut Brussels in two.

For three weeks the men had been on the march and there was not a single straggler, not a strap out of place, not a pennant missing. Along the route, without for a minute halting the machine, the post-office carts fell out of the column, and as the men marched mounted postmen collected postcards and delivered letters. Also, as they marched, the cooks prepared soup, coffee, and tea, walking beside their stoves on wheels, tending the fires, distributing the smoking food. No officer followed a wrong turning, no officer asked his way. He followed the map strapped to his side and on which for his guidance in red ink his route was marked. At night he read this map, by the light of an electric torch buckled to his chest. For the gray automobiles and the gray motorcycles one side of the street always was kept clear; and so compact was the column, so rigid the vigilance of the file-closers, that at the rate of forty miles an hour a car could race the length of the column and need not for a single horse or man once swerve from its course.

To perfect this monstrous engine, with its pontoon bridges, its wireless, its hospitals, its aeroplanes that in rigid alignment sailed before it, its field telephones that as it advanced strung wires over which for miles the vanguard talked to the rear, all modern inventions had been prostituted. To feed it, millions of men had been called from homes, offices, and workshops; to guide it, for years the minds of the highborn, with whom it is a religion and a disease, had been solely concerned.

It is, perhaps, the most efficient organization of modern times; and its purpose only is death. Those who cast it loose upon Europe are military-mad. And they are only a very small part of the German people. But to preserve their class they have in their own image created this terrible engine of destruction. For the present it is their servant. But "Though the mills of God grind slowly, yet they grind exceeding small." And like Frankenstein's monster, this monster, to which they gave live, may turn on them and rend them.

New York Tribune
November 1, 1914

The Appalling Waste of the European War

The Famous American Writer, Who Has Followed Many an Army in Previous Conflicts, Describes the Devastation and Desolation Observed by Him in the Tormented Lands of the Continent

In this war, more than in other campaigns, the wastefulness is apparent. In recent wars, what to the man at home was most distressing was the destruction of life. He measured the importance of the conflict by the daily lists of killed and wounded. But in those wars, except human life, there was little else to destroy. The war in South Africa was fought among hills of stone, across vacant stretches of prairie. Not even trees were destroyed, because there were no trees. In the district over which the armies passed there were not enough trees to supply the men with firewood. In Manchuria, with the Japanese, we marched for miles without seeing even a mud village, and the approaches to Port Arthur were as desolate as our Black Hills. The Italian-Turkish war was fought in the sands of a desert, and in the Balkan war few had heard of the cities bombarded until they read they were in flames. But this war is being waged in that part of the world best known to the rest of the world.

Every summer hundreds of thousands of Americans, on business or on pleasure bent, traveled to the places that now daily are being taken or retaken, or are in ruins. At school they had read of these places in their history book, and later had visited them. In consequence, in this war they have a personal and an intelligent interest. It is as though of what is being destroyed they were part owners.

A Generation of Wasters Has Its First Object Lesson in Waste

Toward Europe they are as absentee landlords. It was their pleasure ground, and their market. And now that it is being laid low the utter wastefulness of war is brought closer to this generation than ever before. Loss of life in war has not been considered entirely wasted, because the self-sacrifice involved ennobled it. And the men who went out to war knew what they might lose. Neither when, in the pursuits of peace, human life is sacrificed is it counted as wasted. The pioneers who were killed by the Indians, or who starved to death in what then were deserts, helped to carry civilization from the Atlantic to the Pacific. Only ten years ago men were killed in learning to control the "horseless wagons," and now 60-horsepower cars are driven by women and young girls. Later the airship took its toll of human life. Nor, in view of the possibilities of the airship in the future, can it be said those lives were wasted. But, except life, there was no other waste. To perfect the automobile and the airship no women were driven from home and the homes destroyed. No churches were bombarded. Men in this country who after many years had built up a trade in Europe were not forced to close their mills and turn into the streets hundreds of working men and women.

The Expanding Kaiser Strikes Far Afield

It is in the by-products of the war that the waste, cruelty and stupidity of war are most apparent. It is the most innocent who suffer and those who have the least offended who are the most severely punished. The German Emperor wanted a place in the sun, and having decided that the right moment to seize it had arrived declared war. As a direct result, Mary Kelly, a telephone girl at the Wistaria Hotel, in New York, is looking for work. It sounds like an O. Henry story, but except for the name of the girl and the hotel it is not fiction. She told me about it yesterday, on Broadway.

"I'm looking for work," she said, "and I thought if you remembered me you might give me a reference. I used to work at Sherry's, and at the Wistaria Hotel. But I lost my job through the war." How the war in Europe could strike at a telephone girl in New York was puzzling, but Mary Kelly made it clear. "The Wistaria is very popular with Southerners," she explained. "They make their money in cotton, and blow it in New York. But now they can't sell their cotton, and so they have no money, and so they can't come to New York. And the hotel is run at a loss, and the proprietor discharged me and the other girl, and the bellboys are tending the switchboard. I've been a month trying to get work. But everybody gives me the same answer. They're cutting down the staff on account of the war. I've walked thirty miles a day looking for a job; and I'm nearly all in. How long do you think this war will last?" This telephone girl looking for work is a tiny by-product of war. She is only one instance of efficiency gone to waste.

Belgium and France Before the Days of Their Desolation

The reader can think of a hundred other instances. In his own life he can show where in his pleasures, his business, in his plans for the future the war has struck at him and has caused him inconvenience, loss or suffering. He can then appreciate how much greater are the loss and suffering to those who live within the zone of fire. In Belgium and France the vacant spaces are very few, and the shells fall among cities and villages lying so close together that they seem to touch hands. For hundreds of years the land has been cultivated, the fields, gardens, orchards tilled and lovingly cared for. The roads date back to the days of Caesar. The stone farmhouses, as well as the stone churches, were built to endure. And for centuries until this war came they had endured. After the battle of Waterloo some of these stone farmhouses found themselves famous. In them Napoleon or Wellington had spread his maps or set up his cot, and until this war the farmhouses of Mont Saint Jean, of Caillou, of Haie Sainte, of the Belle Alliance, remained as they were on the day of the great battle a hundred years ago. They have received no special care, the elements have not spared them, nor caretakers guarded them. They still are used as dwellings, and it was only when you recognized them by having seen them on the postcards that you distinguished them from thousands of other houses, just as old and just as well preserved, that stretched from Brussels to Liege.

But a hundred years after this war those other houses will not be shown on picture postcards. King Albert and his staff may have spent the night in them, but the next day von Kluck and his army passed, and those houses, that had stood for three hundred years, were destroyed. In the papers you have seen many pictures of the shattered roofs, and the streets piled high with fallen walls and lined with gaping cellers, over which once houses stood. The walls can be rebuilt, but what was wasted and which cannot be rebuilt are the labor, the saving, the sacrifices that made those houses not mere walls but homes. A house may be built in a year, or rented overnight; it takes longer than that to make it a home The farmers and peasants in Belgium had spent many hours of many days in keeping their homes beautiful, in making their farms self-supporting. After the work of the day was finished they had planted gardens, had reared fruit trees, built arbors; under them, at meal time, they sat surrounded by those of their own household. To buy the horse and the cow they had pinched and saved; to make the gardens beautiful and the fields fertile they had sweated and slaved, the women as well as the men; even the watchdog by day was a beast of burden.

The Beautiful and the Useful Alike Sacrificed

When in August I reached Belgium between Brussels and Liege the whole countryside showed the labor of these peasants. Unlike the American farmer, they were too poor to buy machines to work for them, and with scythes and sickles in hand they cut the grain; with heavy flails they beat it. All that you saw on either side of the road that was fertile and beautiful was the result of their hard, unceasing, personal effort. Then the war came like a cyclone, and in three weeks the labor of many years was wasted. The fields were torn with shells, the grain was in flames, torches destroyed the villages, by the roadside were the carcasses of the cows that had been killed to feed the invader, and the horses were carried off harnessed to gray gun carriages. These were the things you saw on every side, from Brussels to the German border. The peasants themselves were huddled beneath bridges. They were like vast camps of gypsies, except that, less fortunate than the gypsies, they had lost what he neither possesses nor desires, a home. As the enemy advanced the inhabitants of one village would fly for shelter to the next, only by the shells to be whipped further forward; and so, each hour growing in number, the refugees fled toward Brussels and the coast. They were an army of tramps, of women and children tramps, sleeping in the open fields, beneath the hayricks seeking shelter from the rain, living on the raw turnips and carrots they had plucked from the deserted vegetable gardens. The peasants were not the only ones who suffered. The rich and the noble born were as unhappy and as homeless. They had credit, and in the banks they had money, but they could not get at the money; and when a chateau and a farmhouse are in flames, between them there is little choice.

A Night Scene in Brussels, With War Stripped of Heroics

Three hours after midnight on the day the Germans began their three day's march through Brussels I had crossed the Square Rogier to send a dispatch by one of the many last trains for Ostend. When I returned to the Palace Hotel, seated on the iron chairs on the sidewalk were a woman, her three children and two maidservants. The woman was in mourning which was quite new, for though the war was only a month old many had been killed, among them her husband. The day before, at Tirlemont, shells had destroyed her chateau, and she was on her way to England. She had around her neck two long strings of peals, the maids each held a small handbag, her boy clasped in his arms a forlorn and sleepy fox terrier, and each of the little girls was embracing a bird cage. In one was a canary, in the other a parrot. That was all they had saved. In their way they were just as pathetic as the peasants sleeping under the hedges. They were just as homeless, friendless, just as much in need of food and sleep, and in their eyes was the same look of fear and horror. Bernhardi tells his countrymen that war is glorious, heroic, and for a nation an economic necessity. Instead it is stupid, unintelligent. It creates nothing; it only wastes.

The Losses in Louvain Which No Chronicler Will Ever Record

If it confined itself to destroying forts and cradles of barbed wire then it would be sufficiently hideous. But it strikes blindly, brutally; it tramples on the innocent and the beautiful. It is the bull in the china shop, and the mad dog who snaps at children who are trying only to avoid him. People were incensed at the destruction in Louvain of the library, the Catholic college, the Church of St. Pierre that dated from the thirteenth century. These buildings belonged to the world, and over their loss the world was rightfully indignant, but in Louvain there were also shops and manufactures, hotels and private houses. Each belonged, not to the world, but to one family. These individual families made up a city of 45,000 people. In two days there was not a roof left to cover one of them. The trade those people had built up had been destroyed, the "goodwill and fixings," the stock on the shelves and in the storeroom, the goods in the shop windows, the portraits in the drawing room, the souvenirs and family heirlooms, the love letters, the bride's veil, the baby's first worsted shoes, and the will by which someone bequeathed to his beloved wife all his worldly goods.

War came and sent all these possessions, including the will and the worldly goods, up into the air in flames. Most of the people of Louvain made their living by manufacturing church ornaments and brewing beer. War was impartial, and destroyed both the beer and the church ornaments. It destroyed also the men who made them, and it drove the women and children into concentration camps. When first I visited Louvain it was a brisk, clean, prosperous city. The streets were spotless, the shop windows and cafes were modern, rich looking, inviting, and her great churches and hotel de ville gave to the city grace and dignity. Ten days later, when I again saw it, Louvain was in darkness, lit only by burning buildings. Rows and rows of streets were lined with black, empty walls. Louvain was a city of the past, another Pompeii, and her citizens were being led out to be shot. The fate of Louvain was the fate of Vise, of Malines, of Tirlemont, of Liege, of hundreds of villages and towns, and by the time this is printed it will be the fate of hundreds of other towns over all of Europe.

In this war the waste of horses is appalling. Those that first entered Brussels with the German army had been bred and trained for the purposes of war, and they were magnificent specimens. Every one who saw them exclaimed ungrudgingly in admiration. But by the time the army reached the approaches of Paris the forced marches had so depleted the stock of horses that for remounts the Germans were seizing all they met. Those that could not keep up were shot. For miles along the road from Meaux to Soissons and Rheims their bodies tainted the air.

Horses are Killed Because of Their Possible Usefulness

They had served their purposes, and after six weeks of campaigning the same animals that in times of peace would have proved faithful servants for many years were destroyed, that they might not fall into the hands of the French. Just as an artilleryman spikes his gun, the Germans on their retreat to the Aisne River left in their wake no horse that might assist in their pursuit. As they withdrew they searched each stable yard and killed the horses. In village after village I saw horses lying in the stalls or in the fields still wearing the harness of the plough, or in groups of three or four in the yard of a barn, each with a bullet hole in its temple. They were killed for fear they might be useful.

Waste can go no further. Another example of waste were the motor trucks and automobiles. When the war began the motor trucks of the big department stores and manufacturers and motor buses of London, Paris and Berlin were taken over by the different armies. They had cost them from $2,000 to $3,000 each, and in times of peace had they been used for the purposes for which they were built would several times over have paid for themselves But war gave them no time to pay even for their tires. You saw them by the roadside, cast aside like empty cigarette boxes. A few hours' tinkering would have set them right. They were still good for years of service. But an army in retreat or in pursuit has no time to waste in repairing motors. To waste the motor is cheaper.

Between Villers-Cotterets and Soissons the road was strewn with high power automobiles and motor trucks that the Germans had been forced to destroy. Something had gone wrong, something that at other times could easily had been mended. But with the French in pursuit there was no time to pause, nor could cars of such value be left to the enemy. So they had been set on fire or blown up or allowed to drive head-on into a stone wall or over an embankment. From the road above we could see them in the field below, lying like giant turtles on their backs. In one place in the forest of Villers was a line of fifteen trucks, each capable of carrying five tons. The gasoline to feed them had become exhausted, and the whole fifteen had been set on fire. In war this is necessary, but it was none the less waste. When an army takes the field it must consider first its own safety; and to embarrass the enemy everything else must be sacrificed. It cannot consider the feelings or pockets of railroad or telegraph companies. It cannot hesitate to destroy a bridge because that bridge cost $500,000. And it does not hesitate.

Motoring from Paris to the front these days is a question of avoiding roads rendered useless because a broken bridge has cut them in half. All over France are these bridges of iron, of splendid masonry, some decorated with statues, some dating back hundreds of years, but now with a span blown out, or entirely destroyed and sprawling in the river. All of these material things—motor cars, stone bridges, railroad tracks, telegraph lines—can be replaced. Money can restore them. But money cannot restore the noble trees of France and Belgium, eighty years old or more, that shaded the roads, that made beautiful the parks and forests. For military purposes they have been cut down, or by artillery fire shattered into splinters. They will again grow, but eighty years is a long time to wait.

Losses Which are Unthinkable;
Numbers That are Only Numbers

Nor can money replace the greatest waste of all—the waste in "killed, wounded and missing." The waste of human life in this war is so enormous, so far beyond our daily experience, that disasters less appalling are much easier to understand. The loss of three people in an automobile accident comes nearer home than the fact that at the battle of Sezanne thirty thousand men were killed. Few of us are trained to think of men in such numbers. Certainly not of dead men in such numbers. We have seen thirty thousand men together only during the world's series, or at the championship football matches. To get an idea of the waste of this war we must imagine all of the spectators at a football match between Yale and Harvard suddenly stricken dead. We must think of all the wives, children, friends affected by the loss of those thirty thousand, and we must multiply those thirty thousand by hundreds, and imagine these hundreds of thousands lying dead in Belgium, in Alsace-Lorraine and within ten miles of Paris. After the Germans were repulsed at Meaux and at Sezanne the dead of both armies were so many that they lay intermingled in layers three and four deep. They were buried in long pits and piled on top of each other like cigars in a box. Lines of fresh earth so long that you mistook them for trenches intended to conceal regiments were in reality graves. Some bodies lay for days uncovered until they had lost all human semblance. They were so many you ceased to regard them even as corpses. They had become just a part of the waste, a part of the shattered walls, uprooted trees and fields ploughed by shells. What once had been your fellow men were only bundles of clothes, swollen and shapeless, like scarecrows stuffed with rags, polluting the air.

"The Giving Over of a Game That Must Be Lost"

The wounded were hardly less pitiful. They were so many and so thickly did they fall that the ambulance service at first was not sufficient to handle them. They lay in the fields or forests sometimes for a day before they were picked up suffering unthinkable agony. And after they were placed in cars and started back toward Paris the tortures continued. Some of the trains of wounded that arrived outside the city had not been opened in two days. The wounded had been without food or water. They had not been able to move from the positions in which in torment they had thrown themselves. The foul air had produced gangrene. And when the cars were opened the stench was so fearful that the Red Cross people fell back as though from a blow. For the wounded Paris is full of hospitals— French, English and American. And the hospitals are full of splendid men. Each one once had been physically fit, or he would not have been passed to the front, and those among them who are officers are finely bred, finely educated, or they would not be officers. But each matched his good health, his good breeding and knowledge against a broken piece of shell or steel bullet and the shell or bullet won. They always will win. Stephen Crane called a wound "the red badge of courage." It is all of that. And the man who wears that badge has all my admiration. But I cannot help feeling also the waste of it. I would have a standing army for the same excellent reason that I insure my house; but, except in self-defence, no war. For war—and I have seen a lot of it, is waste. And waste is unintelligent.

New York Tribune
November 8, 1914

"Under Fire"—By Richard Harding Davis

*In Six Wars Among a Score of Races
American Writer Has Seen Only Four Men Destitute of Valor*

One cold day on the Aisne, when the Germans had just withdrawn to the east bank and the Allies held the west, the French soldiers built huge bonfires and huddled around them. When the "Jack Johnsons," as they call the 6-inch howitzer shells that strike with a burst of black smoke, began to fall, sooner than leave the warm fires the soldiers accepted the chance of being hit by the shells. Their officers had to order them back. I saw this and wrote of it. A friend refused to credit it. He said it was against his experience. He did not believe that, for the sake of keeping warm, men would chance being killed.

But the incident was quite characteristic. In times of war you constantly see men, and women, too, who, sooner than suffer discomfort or even inconvenience, risk death. The psychology of the thing is, I think, that a man knows very little about being dead, but has a very acute knowledge of what it is to be uncomfortable. His brain is not able to grasp death, but it is quite capable of informing him that his fingers are cold. Often men receive credit for showing coolness and courage in times of danger, when, in reality, they are not properly aware of the danger and through habit are acting authentically. The girl in Chicago who went back into the Iroquois Theatre fire to rescue her rubber overshoes was not a heroine. She merely lacked imagination. Her mind was capable of appreciating how serious for her would be the loss of her overshoes, but not of being burned alive. At the battle of Velestinos in the

Greek-Turkish war, John F. Bass, of "The Chicago Daily News," and myself got into a trench at the foot of a hill on which later the Greeks placed a battery. All day the Turks bombarded this battery with a cross fire of shrapnel and rifle bullets which did not touch our trench, but cut off our return to Velestinos. Sooner than pass through this cross fire, all day we crouched in the trench until about sunset, when it came on to rain. We exclaimed with dismay. We had neglected to bring our ponchos. "If we don't get back to the village at once," we assured each other, "we will get wet!" So we raced through half a mile of falling shells and bullets and, before the rain fell, got under cover. Then Bass said: "For twelve hours we stuck to that trench because we were afraid if we left it we would be killed. And the only reason we ever did leave it was because we were more afraid of catching cold!"

Cigarettes Routed from His Mind All Thought of Peril

In the same war I was in a trench with some infantrymen, one of whom never raised his head. Whenever he was ordered to fire he would shove his rifle barrel over the edge of the trench, shut his eyes and pull the trigger. He took no chances. His comrades laughed at him and swore at him, but he would only grin sheepishly and burrow deeper. After several hours a friend in another trench held up a bag of tobacco and some cigarette papers and in pantomine "dared" him to come for them. To the intense surprise of every one he scrambled out of our trench and, exposed against the skyline, walked to the other trench and, while he rolled a handful of cigarettes, drew the fire of the enemy. It was not that he was brave; he had shown that he was not. He was merely stupid. Between death and cigarettes, his mind could not rise above cigarettes.

Why the same kind of people are so differently affected by danger is very hard to understand. It is almost impossible to get a line on it. I was in the city of Rheims for three days and two nights while it was being bombarded. During that time fifty thousand people remained in the city and, so far as the shells permitted, continued about their business. The other fifty thousand fled from the city and camped out along the road to Paris. For five miles outside Rheims they lined both edges of that road like people waiting for a circus parade. With them they brought rugs, blankets and loaves of bread, and from daybreak until night fell and the shells ceased to fall they sat in the hay fields and along the grass gutters of the road. Some of them were most intelligent looking and had the manner and clothes of the rich. There was one family of five that on four different occasions on our way to and from Paris we saw seated on the ground at a place certainly five miles away from any spot where a shell had fallen. They were all in deep mourning, but as they sat in the hay field around a wicker tea basket and wrapped in steamer rugs they were comic. Their lives were no more valuable than those of thousands of their fellow townsfolk who in Rheims were carrying on the daily routine. These kept the shops open, or in the streets were assisting the Red Cross.

One elderly gentleman told me how he had been seized by the Germans as a hostage and threatened with death by hanging. With forty other first citizens, from the 4th to the 12th of September he had been in jail. After such an experience one would have thought that between himself and the Germans he would have placed as many miles as possible, but instead he was strolling around the Place du Parvis Notre-Dame in front of the Cathedral. For the French officers who, on sightseeing bent, were motoring into Rheims from the battle line, he was acting as a sort of guide. Pointing with his umbrella, he would say "On the left is the new Palace of Justice, the façade entirely destroyed; on the right you see the palace of the Archbishop, completely wrecked. The shells that just passed over us have apparently fallen in the garden of the Hotel Lion d'Or." He was as cool as the conductor on a "Seeing Rheims" observation car.

He was matched in coolness by our consul, William Bardel. The American Consulate is at No. 14 Rue Kellerman. That morning a shell had hit the chestnut tree in the garden of his neighbor at No. 12 and had knocked all the chestnuts into the garden of the consulate. "It's an ill wind that blows nobody good," said Mr. Bardel.

In the bombarded city there was no rule as to how anyone would act. One house would be closed and barred and the inmates would be either in their own cellar or in the caves of the nearest champagne company. To those latter they would bring books or playing cards and among millions of dust-covered bottles by candlelight would wait for the guns to cease. Their neighbors sat in their shops or stood at the doors of their houses or paraded the streets. Past them their friends were hastening, trembling with terror. Many women sat on the front steps knitting and with interested eyes watched their acquaintances fleeing towards the Paris gate. When overhead a shell passed they would stroll, still knitting, out into the middle of the street to see where the shell struck.

By the noise it was quite easy to follow the flight of the shells. You were tricked by the sound into almost believing you could see them. The six-inch shells passed with a whistling roar that was quite terrifying. It was as though just above you invisible telegraph wires had dangled, and their rush through the air was like the roar that rises to the car window when two express trains going in opposite directions pass at sixty miles an hour. When these sounds assailed them the people flying from the city would scream. Some of them, as though they had been hit, would fall on their knees. Others were sobbing and praying aloud. The tears rolled down their cheeks. In their terror there was nothing ludicrous; they were in as great physical pain as were some of the hundreds in Rheims who had been hit. And yet others of their fellow townsmen living in the same street, and with the same allotment of brains and nerves, were treating the bombardment with the indifference they would show to a summer shower.

We had not expected to spend the night in Rheims, so, with Ashmead Bartlett, the military expert of "The London Daily Telegraph," I went into a chemist's shop to buy some soap. The chemist, seeing I was an American, became very much excited. He was overstocked with an American shaving soap and he begged me to take it off his hands. He would let me have it at what it cost him. He did not know where he had placed it and he was in great alarm lest we would leave his shop before he could unload it on us. From both sides of the town French artillery were firing in salvos, the shocks shaking the air; over the shop of the chemist shrapnel was whining, and in the street the howitzer shells were opening up subways. But his mind was intent only on finding that American shaving soap. I was anxious to get on to a more peaceful neighborhood. To French soap, to soap "made in Germany," to neutral American soap I was indifferent. Had it not been for the presence of Ashmead Bartlett I would have fled. To die, even though clasping a cake of American soap, seemed less attractive than to live unwashed. But the chemist had no time to consider shells. He was intent only on getting rid of surplus stock.

The majority of people who are afraid are those who refuse to consider the Doctrine of Chances. The chances of their being hit may be one in ten thousand, but they disregard the odds in their favor and fix their minds on that one chance against them. In their imagination it grows larger and larger. It looms red, and bloodshot it hovers over them; wherever they go it follows, menacing, threatening, filling them with terror. In Rheims there were 100,000 people, and by shells one thousand were killed or wounded. The chances against were a hundred to one. Those who left the city undoubtedly thought the odds were not good enough.

That One Chance in Million Impressed Them Heavily

Those who on account of the bombs that fell from the German aeroplanes into Paris left that city had no such excuse. The chance of any one person being hit by a bomb was one in several millions. But even with such generous odds in their favor, during the days the bomb dropping lasted many thousands fled. They were obsessed by that one chance against them. In my hotel in Paris my landlady had her mind fixed on that one chance, and regularly every afternoon when the aeroplanes were expected she would go to bed. Just as regularly her husband would take a pair of opera glasses and in the Rue de la Paix hopefully scan the sky.

One afternoon while we waited in front of Cook's an aeroplane sailed overhead, but so far above us that no one knew whether it was a French airship scouting or a German one preparing to launch a bomb. A man from Cook's, one of the interpreters, with a horrible knowledge of English, said: "Taube or not Taube, that is the question." He was told he was inviting a worse death than from a bomb. To illustrate the attitude of mind of the Parisian, there is the story of the street gamin who for some time from the Garden of the Tuileries had been watching a German aeroplane threatening the city. Finally he exclaimed impatiently:

"Oh, throw your bomb! You are keeping me from my dinner."

A soldier under fire furnishes few of the surprises of conduct to which the civilian treats you. The soldier has no choice. He is tied by the leg, and whether the chances are even or ridiculously in his favor he must accept them. The civilian can always say "This is no place for me," and get up and walk away. But the soldier cannot say that. He and his officers, the Red Cross nurses, doctors, ambulance bearers, and even the correspondents have taken some kind of oath or signed some kind of contract that makes it easier for them than for the civilians to stay on the job. For them it would require more courage to go away than to remain.

Indeed, although courage is so highly regarded, it seems to be of all virtues the most common. In six wars, among men of nearly every race, color, religion and training,

I have seen but four men who failed to show courage. I have seen men who were scared, sometimes whole regiments, but they still fought on; and that is the highest courage, for they were fighting both a real enemy and an imaginary one.

There is a story of a certain politician general of our army, who under a brisk fire turned on one of his staff and cried:

"Why, major, you are scared, sir; you are scared."

"I am, sir," said the major, with his teeth chattering, "and if you were as scared as I am, you'd be twenty miles in the rear."

In this war the onslaughts have been so terrific and so unceasing, the artillery fire especially has been so entirely beyond human experience, that the men fight in a kind of daze. Instead of arousing fear the tumult acts as an anaesthetic. With forests uprooted, houses smashed about them and unseen express trains hurtling through space above them, they are too stunned to be afraid. And in time they become fed up on battles, and to the noise and danger grow callous. On the Aisne I saw an artillery battle that stretched for fifteen miles. Both banks of the river were wrapped in smoke; from the shells villages miles away were in flames, and two hundred yards in front of us the howitzer shells were bursting in black fumes. To this the French soldiers were completely indifferent. The hills they occupied had been held that morning by the Germans, and the trenches and fields were strewn with their accoutrement. So all the French soldiers who were not serving the guns wandered about seeking souvenirs. They had never a glance for the villages burning crimson in the bright sunlight or for the falling "Jack Johnsons." They were intent only on finding a spiked helmet, and when they came upon one they would give a shout of triumph and hold it up for their comrades to see. And their comrades would laugh delightedly and race toward them, stumbling over the furrows. They were as happy and eager as children picking wild flowers.

Regain Their Mental Balance with Football and Cards

It is not good for troops to sup entirely on horrors and also to breakfast and lunch on them. So after in the trenches one regiment has been pounded it is withdrawn for a day or two and kept in reserve. The English Tommies spend this period of recuperating in playing football and cards. When the English learned this they forwarded so many thousands of packs of cards to the distributing depot that the War Office had to request them not to send any more. When the English officers are granted leave of absence they do not waste their energy on football, but motor into Paris for a bath and lunch. At eight they leave the trenches along the Aisne and by noon arrive at Maxim's, Voisin's or La Rue's. Seldom does warfare present a sharper contrast. From a breakfast of "bully" beef, eaten from a tin plate, within their nostrils the smell of camp fires, dead horses and unwashed bodies, they find themselves seated on red velvet cushions, surrounded by mirrors and walls of white and gold, and spread before them the most immaculate silver, linen and glass. And the odors that assail them are those of truffles, white wine and *artechant sauce mousseline.*

It is a delight to hear them talk. Their point of view is so sane and fair. In risking their legs or arms, or life itself, they see nothing heroic, dramatic or extraordinary. They talk of the war as they would of a cricket match or a day in the hunting field. If things are going wrong they do not whine or blame, or when fortune smiles are they unduly jubilant. And they are so appallingly honest and frank. A piece of shrapnel had broken the arm of one of them, and we were helping him to cut up his food and pour out his Scotch and soda. Instead of making a hero or a martyr of himself, he said confidingly: "You know, I had no right to be hit. If I had been minding my own business I wouldn't have been hit. But Jimmie was having a hell of a time on top of a hill and I just ran up to have a look in. And the beggars got me. Served me jolly well right, what?"

The Brother Who Accommodatingly Got Himself Shot

I met one subaltern at La Rue's who had been given so many commissions by his brother officers to bring back tobacco, soap and underclothes that all his money save five francs was gone. He still had two days' leave of absence and, as he truly pointed out, in Paris even in wartime five francs will not carry you far. I offered to be his banker, but he said he would first try elsewhere. The next day I met him on the boulevards and asked what kind of a riotous existence he found possible on five francs

"I've had the most extraordinary luck," he said. "After I left you I met my brother. He was just in from the front, and I got all his money."

"Won't your brother need it?" I asked.

"Not at all," said the subaltern cheerfully, "He's shot in the legs and they've put him to bed. Rotten luck for him, you might say, but how lucky for me!"

Had he been the brother who was shot in both legs he would have treated the matter just as light-heartedly.

Our English major, before he reached his own firing line, was hit by a bursting shell in three places. While he was lying in the American ambulance hospital at Neuilly the doctor said to him:

"This cot next to yours is the only one vacant. Would you mind if we put a German in it?"

"By no means," said the major, "I haven't seen one yet."

The stories the English officers told us at La Rue's and Maxim's by contrast with the surroundings were all the more gruesome. Seeing them there it did not seem possible that in a few hours these same fit, sun-tanned youths in khaki would be back in the trenches, or scouting in advance of them, or that only the day before they had been dodging death and destroying their fellow men.

Maxim's, which now reminds one only of the last act of "The Merry Widow," was the meeting place for the French and English officers from the front, the American military attachés from our embassy, among whom were soldiers, sailors, aviators, marines; the doctors and volunteer nurses from the American ambulance, and the correspondents who by night dined in Paris and by day dodged arrest and other things on the firing line, or as near it as they could motor without going to jail. For these Maxim's was the clearing house for news of friends and battles. Where once were the supper girls and ladies of the gold mesh vanity bags now were only men in red and blue uniforms, men in khaki, men in bandages. Among them were English lords and French princes with titles that dated from Agincourt to Waterloo, where their ancestors had met as enemies. Now those who had succeeded them as allies were over a *sole Marguery*, discussing airships, armored automobiles and *mitrailleuses*.

At one table Hugo Frasier, of the American Embassy, would be telling an English officer that a captain of his regiment who was supposed to have been killed at Courtrai had, like a homing pigeon, found his way to the hospital at Neuilly and wanted to be reported "safe" at Lloyds. At one table a French lieutenant would describe a raid made by the son of an American banker in Paris, who is in command of an armored automobile. "He swept his gun only once—so," the Frenchman explained, waving his arm across the champagne and the broiled lobster, "and he caught a general and two staff officers. He cut them in half." Or at another table you would listen to a group of English officers talking in wonder of the German's wasteful advance in solid formation.

"They were piled so high," one of them relates, "that I stopped firing. They looked like gray worms squirming about in a bait box. I can shoot men coming at me on their feet, but not a mess of arms and legs."

"I know," assents another; "when we charged the other day we had to advance over the Germans that fell the night before, and my men were slipping and stumbling all over the place. The bodies didn't give them any foothold."

"My sergeant yesterday," another relates, "turned to me and said: 'It isn't cricket. There's no game in shooting into a target as big as that. It's just murder.' I had to order him to continue firing."

They tell it without pose or emotion. It is all in the day's work. Most of them are young men of wealth, of ancient family, cleanly bred gentlemen of England, and as they nod and leave the restaurant we know that in three hours, wrapped in a greatcoat, each will be sleeping in the earth trenches, and that the next morning the shells will wake them.

New York Tribune
November 15, 1914

Uncle Sam's Diplomats in War Zone Do Him Honor

Famous War Correspondent Tells of Crises Met Sturdily and Wisely by Representatives of This Nation in the Writhing Lands of Europe

When the war broke loose those persons in Europe it concerned the least were the most upset about it. They were our fellow countrymen. Even today, above the roar of shells, the crash of falling walls, forts, forests, cathedrals, above the scream of shrapnel, the sobs of widows and orphans, the cries of the wounded and dying all over Europe, you can still hear the shrieks of the Americans calling for their lost suitcases.

For some of the American women caught by the war on the wrong side of the Atlantic the situation was serious and distressing. There were thousands of them travelling alone, chaperoned only by a man from Cook's, or a letter of credit. For years they had been saving to make this trip, and had allowed themselves only sufficient money after the trip was completed to pay the ship's stewards. Suddenly they found themselves facing the difficulties of existence in a foreign land without money, friends or credit. During the first days of mobilization they could not realize on their checks or letters. American banknotes and Bank of England notes were refused. Save gold, nothing was of value, and everyone who possessed a gold piece, especially if he happened to be a banker, was clinging to it with the desperation of a dope fiend clutching his last pill of cocaine. We can imagine what it was like in Europe when we recall the problems at home.

Banks Refused to Give Gold or Letters of Credit

In New York when I started for the seat of war three banks in which for years I had kept a modest balance refused me a hundred dollars in gold or a check or a letter of credit. They simply put up the shutters and crawled under the bed. So in Europe, where there actually was war, the women tourists, with nothing but a worthless letter of credit between them and sleeping in a park, had every reason to be panic-stricken. But to explain the hysteria of the hundred thousand other Americans is difficult. So difficult that while they live they will still be explaining. The worst that could have happened to them was temporary discomfort, offset by adventures. Of those they experienced they have not yet ceased boasting.

On August 5, one day after England declared war, the American government announced that it would send the *Tennessee* with a cargo of gold. In Rome and in Paris Thomas Nelson Page and Myron T. Herrick were assisting every American who applied to them, and committees of Americans to care for their fellow countrymen had been organized. All that was asked of the stranded Americans was to keep cool and like true sports suffer inconvenience. Around them were the French and English, facing the greatest tragedy of centuries and meeting it calmly and with noble self-sacrifice. The men were marching to meet death, and in the streets, shops and fields the women were taking up the burden the men had dropped. And in the Rue Scribe and in Cockspur Street thousands of Americans were struggling in panic-stricken groups, bewailing the loss of a hot box and protesting at having to return home second class. Their suffering was something terrible. In London in the Ritz and Carlton restaurants American refugees loaded down with fat pearls and seated at tables loaded with fat food, besought your pity. The imperial suite, which on the fast German liner was always reserved for them, "except when Prince Henry was

using it," was no longer available, and they were subjected to
the indignity of returning home on a nice day boat and in the
captain's cabin. It made their blue blood boil; and the thought
that their emigrant ancestors had come over in the steerage did
not help a bit.

Experiences of Judge Irwin And His Party

The experiences of Judge Richard William Irwin, of the
Superior Court of Massachusetts, and his party, as related in
"The Paris Herald," were heartrending. On leaving Switzerland
for France they were forced to carry their own luggage, all
the porters apparently having selfishly marched off to die for
their country, and the train was not lighted, nor did anyone
collect their tickets. "We have them yet!" says Judge Irwin. He
makes no complaint, he does not write to the Public Service
Commission about it, but he states the fact. No one came to
collect his ticket and he has it yet. Something should be done.
Merely because France is at war Judge Irwin should not be
condemned to go through life clinging to a first class ticket.

In another interview Judge George A. Carpenter, of the
United States Court of Chicago, takes a more cheerful view. "I
can't see anything for Americans to get hysterical about," he
says. "They seem to think their little delays and difficulties are
more important than all the troubles of Europe. For my part,
I should think these people would be glad to settle down in
Paris." A wise judge!

For the hysterical Americans it was fortunate that in
the embassies and consulates of the United States there were
fellow countrymen who would not allow a war to rattle them.
When the representatives of other countries fled our people
not only stayed on the job but held down the jobs of those
who were forced to move away. At no time in many years
have our diplomats and consuls appeared to such advantage.
They deserve so much credit that the administration will
undoubtedly try to borrow it. Mr. Bryan will point with pride

and say, "These men who bore themselves so well were my appointments." Some of them were. But back of them, and coaching them, were first and second secretaries, and consuls general and consuls who had been long in the service and who knew the language, the short cuts and what ropes to pull. And they had also the assistance of every lost and strayed, past and present American diplomat who, when the war broke, was caught off his base. These were commandeered and put to work, and volunteers of the American colonies were made honorary attachés, and without pay toiled like $15-a-week bookkeepers.

In our embassy in Paris one of these latter had just finished struggling with two American women. One would not go home by way of England because she would not leave her Pomeranian in quarantine and the other because she could not carry with her twenty-two trunks. They demanded to be sent back from Havre on a battleship. The volunteer diplomat bowed. "Then I must refer you to our naval attaché, on the first floor," he said. "Any tickets for battleships must come through him."

I suggested he was having a hard time.

"If we remained in Paris," he said, "we all had to help. It was a choice between volunteering to aid Mr. Herrick at the embassy, or Mrs. Herrick at the American Ambulance Hospital and tending wounded Turcos. But between soothing terrified Americans and washing niggers, I'm sorry now I didn't choose the hospital."

Two Embassies Running Overtime In Paris

In Paris there were two embassies running overtime; that means from early morning until after midnight, and each with a staff enlarged to six times the usual number. At the residence of Mr. Herrick, in the Rue Francois Ier, there was an impromptu staff composed chiefly of young American bankers, lawyers and businessmen. They were men who inherited or who earned incomes of from twenty thousand to fifty thousand a year, and all day and every day without pay, and certainly without thanks, they assisted their bewildered, penniless and homesick fellow countrymen. Below them in the cellar was stored part of the $2,500,000 voted by Congress to assist the stranded Americans. It was guarded by quick-firing guns loaned by the French War Office and by six petty officers from the *Tennessee*. With one of them I had been a shipmate when the *Utah* sailed from Vera Cruz. I congratulated him on being in Paris.

"They say Paris is some city," he assented, "but all I've seen of it is this courtyard. Don't tell anybody, but, on the level, I'd rather be back in Vera Cruz!"

The work of distributing the money was carried on in the chancelleries of the embassy in the Rue de Chaillot. It was entirely in the hands of American army and navy officers, twenty of whom came over on the warship with Assistant Secretary of War Breckinridge. Major Spencer Cosby, the military attaché of the embassy, was treasurer of the fund, and every application for aid that had not already been investigated by the civilian committee appointed by the ambassador was decided upon by the officers. Mr. Herrick found them invaluable. He was earnest in their praise. They all wanted to see the fighting; but in other ways they served their country. As a kind of "King's messenger" they were sent to our other embassies, to the French government at Bordeaux and in command of expeditions to round up and convoy back to Paris stranded Americans in Germany and Switzerland. Their training, their habit of command and of thinking for others, their military titles, helped them to success. By the French they were given a free road, and they were not only of great assistance to others, but what they saw of the war and of the French army will be of lasting benefit to themselves. Among them were officers of every branch of the army and navy, and of the marine and aviation corps. Their reports to the War Department, if ever they are made public, will be mighty interesting reading.

Line in Front of Embassy Never Seemed To End

The regular staff of the embassy was occupied not only with Americans, but with English, Germans and Austrians. These latter stood in a long line outside the embassy herded by gendarmes. That line never seemed to grow less. Myron T. Herrick, our ambassador, was at the embassy from early in the morning until midnight. He was always smiling, helpful, tactful, optimistic. Before the war came he was already popular; and the manner in which he met the dark days when the Germans were within fifteen miles of Paris made him thousands of friends. He never asked any of his staff to work harder than he worked himself, and he never knocked off and called it a day's job before they did. Nothing seemed to worry or daunt him; neither the departure of the other diplomats when the government moved to Bordeaux and he was left alone, nor the advancing Germans and threatened siege of Paris, nor even falling bombs.

Herrick was as democratic as he was efficient. For his exclusive use there was a magnificent audience chamber full of tapestry, ormolu brass, Sevres china and sunshine. But of its grandeur the ambassador would grow weary, and every quarter hour he would come out into the hall crowded with waiting English and Americans. There, assisted by Mr. Charles, who is as invaluable to our ambassadors to France as are Frank and Edward Hodson to our ambassadors to London, he would hold an impromptu reception. It was interesting to watch the ex-governor of Ohio clear that hall and send everybody away smiling. Having talked to his ambassador instead of to a secretary, each went off content. In the hall one morning I found a noble lord of high degree chuckling with pleasure.

"This is the difference between your ambassadors and ours," he said. "An English ambassador won't let you in to see him; your American ambassador comes out to see you."

However true that may be, it was extremely fortunate that when war came we should have had a man at the storm centre so admirably efficient.

Our embassy was not embarrassed, nor was it greatly helped by the presence in Paris of two other American ambassadors: Mr. Sharp, the ambassador-elect, and Mr. Bacon, an ambassador that was. That at such a crisis these gentlemen should have chosen to come to Paris and remain there showed that for an ambassador tact is not absolutely necessary.

Mr. Herrick Fortunate in His Secretaries

Mr. Herrick was exceedingly fortunate in his secretaries, Robert Woods Bliss and Arthur H. Frazier. Their training in the diplomatic service made them most valuable. With him, also, as a volunteer counsellor, was H. Perceval Dodge, who, after serving in diplomatic posts in six countries, was thrown out of the service to make room for a lawyer from Daville, Ky. Dodge was sent over to assist in distributing the money voted by Congress, and Herrick, knowing his record, signed him on to help him in the difficult task of running the affairs of the embassies of four countries, three of which were at war. Dodge, Bliss and Frazier were able to care for these embassies because, though young in years, in the diplomatic service they have had training and experience. In this crisis they proved the need of it. For the duties they were, and still are, called upon to perform it is not enough that a man should have edited a democratic newspaper or stumped the state of Bryan. A knowledge of languages, of foreign countries and of foreigners, their likes and their prejudices, good manners, tact and training, may not in the eyes of the administration seem necessary, but in helping the 90,000,000 people in whose interest the diplomat is sent abroad these qualifications are not insignificant.

One might say that Brand Whitlock, who is so splendidly holding the fort at Brussels, in the very centre of the conflict, is not a trained diplomat. But he started with an excellent knowledge of the French language, and during the eight years in which he was mayor of Toledo he must have learned something of diplomacy, responsibility and of the way to handle men, even German military governors. He is in fact the right man in the right place. In Belgium all men, Belgians, Americans, Germans, speak well of him. In one night he shipped out of Brussels in safety and comfort 5,000 Germans; and when the German army advanced upon that city it was largely due to him and to the Spanish Minister, the Marques Villalabor, that Brussels did not meet the fate of Antwerp. He has a direct way of going at things. One day while the Belgian government still was in Brussels and Whitlock in charge of the German legation, the chief justice called upon him. It was suspected, he said, that on the roof of the German legation, concealed in the chimney, was a wireless outfit. He came to suggest that the American minister, representing the German interests, and the chief justice should appoint a joint commission to investigate the truth of the rumor, to take the testimony of witnesses, and make a report.

"Wouldn't it be quicker," said Whitlock, "if you and I went up on the roof and looked down the chimney?"

Ambassador and Chief Justice Play Detectives

The Chief Justice was surprised but delighted. Together they clambered over the roof of the German legation. They found that the wireless outfit was a rusty weathervane that creaked.

When the government moved to Antwerp, Whitlock asked permission to remain at the capital. He believed that in Brussels he could be of greater service to both Americans and Belgians. And while diplomatic corps moved from Antwerp to Ostend, and from Ostend to Havre, he and Villalabor stuck to their posts. What followed showed Whitlock was right. Today from Brussels he is directing the efforts of the rest of the world to save the people of that city and of Belgium from death by starvation. In this he has the help of his wife, who was Miss Ella Brainerd, of Springfield, Ill.; M. Gaston de Leval, a Belgian gentleman, and Miss Caroline S. Larner, who was formerly a secretary in the State Department, and who, when the war started, was on a vacation in Belgium. She applied to Whitlock to aid her to return home; instead, much to her delight, he made her one of the legation staff. His right hand man is Hugh C. Gibson, his first secretary, a diplomat of experience. It is a pity that to the legation in Brussels no military attaché was accredited. He need not have gone out to see the war, the war would have come to him. As it was, Gibson saw more of actual warfare than did any or all of our twenty-eight military men in Paris. It was his duty to pass frequently through the firing lines on his way to Antwerp and London. He was constantly under fire. Three times his automobile was hit by bullets. These trips were so hazardous that Whitlock urged that he should take them. It is said he and his secretary used to toss for it. Gibson told me he was disturbed by the signs the Germans placed between Brussels and Antwerp, stating that "automobiles looking as though they were on reconnaissance" would be fired upon. He asked how an automobile looked when it was on reconnaissance.

Gibson is one of the few men who, despite years in the diplomatic service, refuses to take himself seriously. He is always smiling, cheerful, always amusing, but when the dignity or his official position is threatened he can be serious enough. When he was charge d'affaires in Havana a young Cuban journalist assaulted him. That journalist is still in jail. In Brussels a German officer tried to blue pencil a cable Gibson was sending to the State Department. Those who witnessed the dent say it was like a buzz saw cutting soft pine.

When the present administration turned out the diplomats it spared the consuls general and consuls. It was fortunate for the State Department that it showed this self-control, and fortunate for thousands of Americans who, when the war cloud burst, were scattered all over Europe. Our consuls rose to the crisis and rounded them up, supplied them with funds, special trains and letters of identification, and when they were arrested rescued them from jail. Under fire from shells and during days of bombardment the American consuls in France and Belgium remained at their posts and protected the people of many nationalities confided to their care. Only one showed the white feather. He first removed himself from his post, and then was removed still further from it by the State Department. All the other American consuls I met or heard of in Belgium, France and England were covering themselves with glory and bringing credit to their country. Nothing disturbed their calm, and at no hour could you catch them idle or reluctant to help a fellow countryman. Their office hours were from 12 to 12, and each consulate had taken out an all-night license and thrown away the key. With four other Americans I was forced to rout one consul out of bed at 2 in the morning. He was Colonel Albert W. Swalm, of Iowa, but of late years our representative at Southampton. That port was in the military zone, and before an American could leave it for Havre it was necessary that his passport should be vised in London by the French and Belgian consuls general and in Southampton by Colonel Swalm. We arrived in Southampton at 2 in the morning to learn that the boat left at 4, and that unless, in the interval, we obtained the autograph and seal of Colonel Swalm she would sail without us.

  In the darkness we set forth to seek our consul, and we found that difficult as it was to leave the docks by sea it was just as difficult by land. In wartime 2 o'clock in the morning is no hour for honest men to prowl around wharves. So we were given to understand by very wide awake sentries with bayonets, policemen and enthusiastic special constables. They received us in a way that made trying to force an entrance to the Rockefeller home at Tarrytown as agreeable as reading "Welcome" on a mat. But at last we reached the consulate and laid siege. One man pressed the electric button, kicked the door and pounded with the knocker, others hurled pebbles at the upper windows, and the fifth stood in the road and sang, "Oh, say, can you see, by the dawn's early light."

A policeman came along and arrested us for throwing stones at the consular sign. We explained that we had hit the sign by accident while aiming at the windows, and that in any case it was the inalienable right of Americans to stone their own consul's sign if they felt like it. He said he always had understood we were a free people, but, "without meaning any disrespect to you, sir, throwing stones at your consul's coat of arms is almost, as you might say, sir, making too free." He then told us Colonel Swalm lived in the suburbs, and in a taxicab started us toward him.

Scantily but decorously clad, Colonel Swalm received us and greeted us as courteously as though we had come to present him with a loving cup. He acted as though our pulling him out of bed at 2 in the morning was intended as a compliment. As for affixing the seal to our passports he refused to accept any fee. We protested that the consuls general of all other nations were demanding fees. "I know," he said, "but I have never thought it right to fine a man for being an American."

Of our ambassadors and representatives to countries in Europe other than France and Belgium I have not written, because during this war I have not visited those countries. But of them, also, all men speak well. At the last election one of them was a candidate for the United States senate. He was not elected. The reason is obvious. It is that the people at home are so well pleased with him and our other ambassadors in Europe that while the war continues, they would keep them where they are.

New York Tribune
November 22, 1914

War Correspondents Fight for Place in the Sun

Writer Tells of Hunting, Harassing and Incarcerating of Himself and His Confreres in the War Zones of Europe

The attitude of the newspaper reader toward the war correspondent who tries to supply him with war news is puzzling.

One might be pardoned for suggesting that their interests are the same. If the correspondent is successful, the better service he renders the reader. The more he is permitted to see at the front, the more news he is allowed to cable home, the better satisfied should be the man who follows the war through the "extras."

But what happens is the reverse of that. Never is the "constant reader" so delighted as when the war correspondent gets the worst of it. It is the one sure laugh. The longer he is kept at the base, the more he is bottled up, "deleted," censored and made prisoner, the greater is the delight of the man at home. He thinks the joke is on the war correspondent. I think it is on the "constant reader." If, at breakfast, the correspondent fails to supply the morning paper with news, the reader shrieks his scorn and claims the joke is on the news gatherer. But if the milkman fails to leave the milk, and the baker the rolls, is the joke on the milkman and the baker or is it on the "constant reader"? Which goes hungry?

Which Proves That "Constant Reader" is Quite Human

The explanation of this attitude of the "constant reader" to the reporters seems to be that he regards the correspondent as a prying busybody, as a sort of spy, and when he is snubbed and suppressed he feels he is properly punished. Perhaps the reader also resents the fact that while the correspondent goes abroad, he stops at home and receives the news at second hand. Possibly he envies the man who has a front seat and who tells him about it. And if you envy a man, when that man comes to grief it is only human nature to laugh.

You have seen unhappy small boys outside a baseball park, and one happy boy inside on the highest seat of the grandstand, who calls down to them why the people are yelling and who has struck out. Do the boys on the ground love the boy in the grandstand and are they grateful to him? Not so you would notice it.

Does the fact that they do not love him and are not grateful to him for telling them the news distress the boy in the grandstand? Not so you would notice it. For no matter how closely he is bottled up, how strictly censored, "deleted," arrested, searched and persecuted, as between the man at home and the correspondent, the correspondent will always be the more fortunate. He is watching the march of great events, he is studying history in the making, and all he sees is of interest. Were it not of interest he would not have been sent to report it. He watches men acting under the stress of all the great emotions. He sees them inspired by noble courage, pity, the spirit of self-sacrifice, of loyalty and pride of race and country.

Other Excitements Equal Thrills of Correspondents

In Cuba I saw Captain Robb Church of our army win the Medal of Honor, in South Africa I saw Captain Gray of the Scot Greys win his Victoria Cross. Those of us who watched him knew he had won it just as surely as you know when a runner crosses the home plate and scores. Can the man at home get from the crook play or the home run a thrill that can compare with the sight of a man offering up his life that other men may live?

Since returning to New York every second man I know greets me sympathetically with "So, you had to come home, hey? They wouldn't let you see a thing." And if I have time to tell them all I saw was the German, French, Belgian and English armies in the field, Belgium in ruins and flames, the Germans sacking Louvain, in the Dover Straits dreadnoughts, cruisers, torpedo destroyers, submarines, hydroplanes; in Paris bombs falling from airships and a city put to bed at 9 o'clock; battlefields covered with dead men; fifteen miles of artillery firing across the Aisne at fifteen miles of artillery; the bombardment of Rheims with shells lifting the roofs as easily as you would lift the cover of a chafing dish and digging holes in the streets, and the cathedral on fire; I saw hundreds of thousands of soldiers from India, Senegal, Morocco, Ireland, Australia, Algiers, Bavaria, Prussia, Scotland, saw them marching over the whole northern half of Europe, saw them wounded and helpless, saw thousands of women and children sleeping under hedges and haystacks with on every side of them their homes blazing in flames or crashing in ruins. That was a part of what I saw. What during the same two months did the man at home see? If he were lucky he saw the Braves win the world's series, or the Vernon Castles dance the fox trot.

Present Popularity of War Correspondents in Europe

The war correspondents who were sent to this war knew it was to sound their death knell They knew that because the newspapers that had no correspondents at the front told them so; because the General Staff of each army told them so; because every man they met who stayed at home told them so. Instead of taking their death blow lying down they went out to meet it. In other wars as rivals they had fought to get the news; in this war they were fighting for their professional existence, for their ancient right to stand on the firing line, to report the facts, to try to describe the indescribable. If their death knell sounded they did not hear it. If they were licked they did not know it. In the twenty-five years in which I have followed wars, in no other war have I seen the war correspondents so well prove their right to march with armies. The happy days when they were guests of the army, when news was served to them by the men who made the news, when Archibald Forbes and Frank Millet shared the same mess with the future Czar of Russia, when MacGahan slept in the tent with Skobeleff and Kipling rode with Roberts, have passed. Now, with every army the correspondent is as popular as a floating mine, as welcome as the man dropping bombs from an airship. The hand of everyone is against him. "Keep out! This means you!" is the way they greet him.

Irrepressible Who Had a Faculty for Getting Arrested

Added to the dangers and difficulties they must overcome in any campaign, which are only what give the game its flavor, they are now hunted, harassed and imprisoned. But the new conditions do not halt them. They, too, are fighting for their place in the sun. I know one man whose name in this war has been signed to dispatches as brilliant and numerous as those of any correspondent but which for obvious reasons is not given here. He was arrested by one army, kept four days in a cell and then warned if he was again found within the lines of the army he would go to jail for six months; one month later he was once more arrested and told if he again came near the front he would go to prison for two years. Two weeks later he was back out. Such a story causes the teeth of all the members of the General Staff to gnash with fury. You can hear them exclaiming: "If we caught that man we would treat him as a spy." And so unintelligent are they on the question of correspondents that they probably would.

When Orville Wright hid himself in South Carolina to perfect his flying machine he objected to what he called the "spying" of correspondents. One of them rebuked him. "You have discovered something," he said, "in which the whole civilized world is interested. If it is true you have made it possible for man to fly, that discovery is more important than your personal wishes. Your secret is too valuable for you to keep to yourself. We are not spies. We are civilization demanding to know if you have something that more concerns the whole world than it can possibly concern you."

A Multitude of Questions Met with Silence

As applied to war, that point of view is equally just. The army calls for your father, husband, son—calls for your money. It enters upon a war that destroys your peace of mind, wrecks your business, kills the men of your family, the man you were going to marry, the son you brought into the world. And to you the army says: "This is our war. We will fight it in our own war, and of it you can learn only what we choose to tell you. We will not let you know whether our country is winning the fight or is in danger, whether we have blundered and the soldiers are starving, whether they give their lives gloriously or through our lack of preparation or inefficiency are dying of neglected wounds." And if you answer that you will send with the army men to write letters home and tell you, not the plans for the future and the secrets of the army, but what are already accomplished facts, the army makes reply: "No, those men cannot be trusted. They are spies."

Not for one moment does the army honestly think those men are spies. But it is the excuse nearest to hand. It is the easiest way out of a situation every army, save our own, has failed to treat with intelligence Every army knows that there are men today acting, or anxious to act, as war correspondents who can be trusted absolutely, whose loyalty and discretion are above question, who no more would rob their army of a military secret than they would rob a till. If the army does not know that it is unintelligent. That is the only crime I impute to our general staff—lack of intelligence.

When Captain Granville Fortescue, of the Hearst syndicate, told the French general that his word as a war correspondent was as good as that of any general in any army he was indiscreet, but he was stating a fact. The answer of the French general was to put him in prison. That was not an intelligent answer.

The last time I was arrested was at Romigny, by General Asebert. I had on me a 3,000-word story, written that morning in Rheims, telling of the wanton destruction of the cathedral. I asked the General Staff, for their own good, to let the story go through. It stated only facts which I believed were they known to civilized people would cause them to protest against a repetition of such outrages. To get the story on the wire I made to Lieutenant Lucien Frechet and Major Klotz, of the General Staff, a sporting offer. For every word of my dispatch they censored I offered to give them for the Red Cross of France five francs. That was an easy way for them to subscribe to the French wounded $3,000. To release his story Gerald Morgan, of "The London Daily Telegraph," made them the same offer. It was a perfectly safe offer for Gerald to make, because a great part of his story was an essay on Gothic architecture. They answer was to put both of us in the Cherche-Midi prison. The next day the censor read my story and said to Lieutenant Frechet and Major Klotz: "But I must insist this goes at once. It should have been sent twenty-four hours ago."

Than the courtesy of the French officers nothing could have been more correct, but I submit that when you earnestly wish to help a man to have him constantly put you in prison is confusing. It was all very well to dissemble your love. But why did you kick me downstairs?

There was the case of Luigi Barzini. In Italy Barzini is the D'Annunzio of newspaper writers. Of all Italian journalists he is the best known. On September 18, at Romigny, General Asebert arrested Barzini, and for four days kept him in a cow stable. Except what he begged from the gendarmes, he had no food and he slept on straw. When I saw him at the headquarters of the General Staff under arrest I told them who he was, and that were I in their place I would let him see all there was to see, and let him, as he wished, write to his people of the excellence of the French army and of the inevitable success of the Allies. With Italy balancing on the fence and needing very little urging to cause her to join her fortunes with France, to choose that moment to put Italian journalists in a cow yard struck me as dull.

The Armies Say to the Governments: "Hands Off!"

In this war the foreign offices of the different governments have been willing to allow correspondents to accompany the army. They know that there are other ways of killing a man than by hitting him with a piece of shrapnel. One way is to tell the truth about him. In this entire war nothing hit Germany so hard a blow as the publicity given to a certain remark about a scrap of paper. But from the government the army would not tolerate any interference. It said: "Do you want us to run this war or do you want to run it?" Each army of the Allies treated its own government much as Walter Camp would treat the Yale faculty if it tried to tell him who should play right tackle.

As a result of the ban put upon the correspondents by the armies the English and a few American newspapers, instead of sending into the field one accredited representative, gave their credentials to a dozen. These men had no other credentials. The letter each received stating that he represented a newspaper worked both ways. When arrested it helped to save him from being shot as a spy, and it was almost sure to lead him to jail. The only way we could hope to win out was through the good nature of an officer or his ignorance of the rules. Many officers did not know that at the front correspondents were prohibited.

As in the old days of former wars we would occasionally come upon an officer who was glad to see someone from the base who could tell him the news and carry back from the front messages to his friends and family. He knew we could not carry away from him any information of value to the enemy, because he had none to give. In a battle front extending one hundred miles he knew only his own tiny unit. On the Aisne a general told me the shrapnel smoke we saw two miles away on his right came from the English artillery, and that on his left five miles distant were the Canadians. At that exact moment the English were at Havre and the Canadians were in Montreal.

In order to keep at the front, or near it, we were forced to make use of every kind of trick and expedient. An English officer who was acting as a correspondent, and with whom for several weeks I shared the same automobile, had no credentials except an order permitting him to pass the policemen at the British War Office. With this he made his way over half of France. In the corner of the pass was the seal or coat of arms of the War Office. When a sentry halted him he would with great care and with an air of confidence unfold this permit and with a proud smile point at the red seal. The sentry who could not read English could invariably salute the coat of arms of his ally, and wave us forward.

They Managed to Play One Army Against Another

That we were with allied armies instead of with one was a great help. We would play one against the other. When a French officer halted us we would not show him a French pass but a Belgian one, or one in English, and out of courtesy to his ally he would permit us to proceed. But out greatest asset always was a newspaper. After a man has been in a dirt trench for two weeks absolutely cut off from the entire world, and when that entire world is at war, for a newspaper he will give his shoes and his blanket.

The Paris papers were printed on a single sheet and would pack as close as banknotes. We never left Paris without several hundred of them, but lest we might be mobbed we showed only one. It was the duty of one of us to hold this paper in readiness. The man who was to show the pass sat by the window. Of all our worthless passes our rule was always to show first the one of least value. If that failed we brought out a higher card, and continued until we had reached the ace. If that proved to be a two-spot we all went to jail. Whenever we were halted, invariably there was the knowing individual who recognized us as newspaper men, and in order to save his country from destruction clamored to have us hung. It was for this pest that the one with the newspaper lay in wait. And the instant the pest opened his lips our man in reserve would shove the "Figaro" at him. "Have you seen this morning's paper?" he would ask sweetly. It never failed us. The suspicious one would grab at the paper as a dog snatches at a bone, and our chauffeur, trained to our team, would shoot forward.

A Wearying Game Which Only the Crook Can Understand

When after hundreds of delays we did reach the firing line we always announced we were on our way back to Paris and would convey their postal cards and letters. If you were anxious to stop in any one place this was an excellent excuse. For at once every officer and soldier began writing to the loved ones at home, and while they wrote you knew you would not be molested and were safe to look at the fighting.

It was most wearing, irritating, nerve-racking work. You knew you were on the level. In spite of the General Staff you believed you had a right to be where you were. You knew you had no wish to pry into military secrets; you knew that toward the allied armies you felt only admiration—that you wanted only to help. But no one else knew that; or cared. Every hundred yards you were halted, cross-examined, searched, put through a third degree. It was senseless, silly and humiliating. Only a professional crook with his thumb prints and photograph in every station house can appreciate how from minute to minute we lived. Under such conditions work is difficult. It does not make for efficiency to know that any man you meet is privileged to touch you on the shoulder and send you to prison.

This is a world war, and my contention is that the world has a right to know, not what is going to happen next, but at least what has happened. If men have died nobly, if women and children have cruelly and needlessly suffered, if for no military necessity and without reason cities have been wrecked, the world should know that.

Those who are carrying on this war behind a curtain, who have enforced this conspiracy of silence, tell you that in their good time the truth will be known. It will not. If you doubt this read the accounts of this war sent out from the Yser by the official "eyewitness" or "observer" of the English General Staff. Compare his amiable gossip in early Victorian phrases with the story of the same battle by Percival Phillips; with the description of the fall of Antwerp by Arthur Ruhl, and the retreat to the Marne by Robert Dunn. Some men are trained to fight, and others are trained to write. The latter can tell you of what they have seen so that you, safe at home at the breakfast table, also can see it. Any newspaper correspondent would rather send his paper news than a descriptive story. But news lasts only until you have told it to the next man, and if in this war the correspondent is not to be permitted to send the news I submit he should at least be permitted to tell what has happened in the past. This war is a world enterprise and in it every man, woman and child is an interested stockholder. They have a right to know what is going forward. The directors' meetings should not be held in secret.

Scribner's
January, 1915

Rheims During the Bombardment

We left Paris with the idea of watching from a point south of Soissons the battle then in progress on the Aisne. Our going to Rheims was an after-thought. Ashmead-Bartlett, of the London *Daily Telegraph*, Captain Granville Fortescue, of the Hearst newspapers, Gerald Morgan, of the same syndicate, and I shared the automobile. To Morgan any map is an open book; so we had left it to him to plan our route. He arranged one which, while apparently not intended to lead us to any particular place, would keep us away from Villers-Cotterets.

"Veal cutlets," as the Tommies had christened it, was our dead-line. The officers of the English General Staff had made it their headquarters, and had they been afflicted with leprosy, smallpox, and bubonic plague, we could not have feared them more. Against war correspondents they had declared war to the death. Unless the setting sun did not show a line of correspondents in chains, they considered that day wasted. During that week they had "bagged" thirteen, and the day before we had seen John Reed and Robert Dunn, who had ventured hat in hand into the presence of General Sir Horace Smith-Dorrien, fast in his net, and on their way to the prison at Tours. So, with the English army, although we much desired to follow it, we were taking no chances. Any man in khaki filled us with terror. If we met even a stray Tommie trying to find his way back to his regiment, the chauffeur turned the car and fled.

So, in avoiding Villers-Cotterets, we found ourselves on the hills above the Vesle River, and below us, mounting from the plain like a great fortress, the cathedral of Rheims. From what I had seen of the destruction of Louvain, I did not believe the Germans could for two weeks occupy Rheims and leave the cathedral intact; and I urged that in America there would be more interest in any affront put upon Rheims cathedral than in the result of that day's battle. The others disagreed, but as in the automobile I was a fourth owner, it was arranged that that fourth should go to Rheims and later accompany the other three-fourths to Soissons. What we saw in the cathedral kept us in Rheims. This was on the 18th of September, before the roof caught fire, when the greatest damage the cathedral had suffered was the destruction of her windows, and when it was being used as a hospital for German wounded. On the two towers Red Cross flags were flying.

The wounded lay in the western end of the building, which opens on the square. The praying-chairs that once had filled the nave had been pushed aside and the stone floor was piled knee-deep with loose straw. On this lay the men to the number of sixty. With them was a young lieutenant who was shot through the eyes, and an elderly major, a reservist, who looked less a soldier than a professor. With his back to a stone pillar he sat half-buried in the straw with one hand pressing tight a shattered arm. To protect the privacy of the wounded all the doors had been closed, and the light came only from the windows; and as they are high above the floor, the lower half of the cathedral was in twilight.

To the east were the carved screens, the chapels, tapestries, altars, the brass and silver candlesticks, the statues of the holy family, of saints and angels, of Joan of Arc. To the west was the yellow straw in which lay the gray ghosts nursing bloody bandages. Impartially upon the sacred symbols of the church, and upon the dirt and blood-stained men battered near to death by their fellow men, the famous windows of Rheims shone like vast jewels. For, in spite of the shells, parts of the stained glass still remained, and into the gray shadows cast pointing rays of blue and crimson. But the perfect glory of the glass was gone. Shrapnel and flying bits of masonry had cut through the expanses of deep blue, a blue which is as pure and cold as the blue of a winter sky by moonlight, and in them torn great gashes. Through these wounds you saw the dull sky and the falling rain. In one place in the wall a shell had made a breach so large that through it might have passed a taxicab. In spite of the nature of the building, in spite of the Red Cross flags, the shell had come shrieking into this by-path of the war, and aimed by Germans had killed two of the German wounded. With their toes pointing stiffly, they lay under little mounds of straw, their gray, wax-like hands folded in peace.

We were escorted through the cathedral by the curé doyen of the church of Saint Jacques, Chanoine A. Frézet. His own church up to that time had not greatly suffered; nor was he one of the staff of the cathedral, but, like every other man, woman, and child in Rheims, he felt as though the stained-glass windows belonged to him. He spoke of the loss of them as of the dead.

"Except at Chartres and at Burgos, in Spain," he said, "there was in all the world no glass so beautiful. It was seven hundred years old; and the glass is gone, and the secret of it is gone."

When we saw the havoc caused by the howitzers we had planned at once to carry the story of the desecration of the cathedral back to Paris. But while we still were in the cathedral two French batteries of field-guns from the outskirts of Rheims opened on the German positions across the river, and the Germans again began to bombard the city. As this still further threatened the cathedral, we decided, until we knew the result of the bombardment, to wait. We told our chauffeur to make his headquarters in the square in front of the cathedral. We chose that spot because from every part of Rheims the two towers were visible, and to find our way back appeared easy. We did not then suppose the Germans would make the cathedral their chief target. We walked to the outskirts of the town to watch the French artillery, but the end of each street was blocked with barricades, and through these the French officers would not allow us to pass. To view the work of the German batteries it was not necessary to leave the city. In it the six-inch howitzer shells were now falling fast. They followed each other with the regularity of trolley-cars, and the people were closing the shutters and taking refuge in their cellars, or in the caves of the champagne companies, or through the streets were flying toward the road to Paris. When the shells struck in the street, the heavy stones gave them greater power.

At the battle of Soissons we had watched them fall in the fields, where they had thrown out black fumes and ploughed up the turnips. In the soft soil they were less destructive than picturesque. But, just as it is easier to "line out" a swift ball than a slow one, so, in Rheims, when the shells struck the stone pavements and the brick and stucco houses, their resistance aided the explosive power of the shells and the result was great excavations in the streets and the wiping out of entire buildings. These latter in one second the shells lifted, shook, and deposited in rubbish in the cellar. In other bombardments I have watched a house lose its roof much as a hat is snatched off by the wind, a cornice carried away, windows punched out, and finally the whole structure battered to its knees.

It took time, and you saw the wall, or fort, or house disintegrate. But these six-inch German howitzer shells do not dismember; they destroy. It was like a gigantic conjuring trick. Over your head an invisible express train swept through space; in front of you a house disappeared. Except for those who were escaping, and the infantry who guarded the town, the streets were empty. The infantry told us they had just returned from Belgium. They were lean, tanned, clear-eyed. In spite of their long "hike" they were neither footsore nor weary. Instead, they were extremely fit and cheerful. They disregarded the shells entirely; and were moving from house to house inquiring anxiously for any cigarettes the Germans might have overlooked.

The shells had been falling near the cathedral; and when we returned to the square we did not expect to find our chauffeur. And, as it turned out, save for the statue of Joan of

Arc, the square was empty. A sentry ran from one of the portals of the church and told us the chauffeur had arranged with himself to meet us outside the gate to Paris. He had waited, the sentry explained, until two houses within a hundred yards of him had vanished, then he, too, had vanished. In the Rue de Vesle we joined the stream of people making toward the city gate. They formed only a small part of the population. The rest of Rheims was standing in the doors, or on the sidewalk, watching those who fled. Those who had elected to remain did not appear disturbed. Young people, arm in arm, were parading the street, searching the sky for air-ships, pointing eagerly when a column of black smoke or powdered cement marked where a shell had burst.

At the gate of the city we asked if anyone had seen our car. A man in a blouse had not seen it; but he knew how we could find it. We had only to accompany him to the general staff, who were occupying the gendarmerie. If there were any people we were less anxious to meet than the general staff it was the gendarmes. We tried to escape from the man in the blouse.

Whether he was a secret agent who thought we were spies, or the village pest, we could not tell; but he would not leave us. We whispered to each other and in the crowd lost ourselves. But the man in the blouse, accompanied by a policeman, pursued. The captain of gendarmes desired to speak with us. We knew what that meant. It meant showing our papers, which would disclose the damning fact that we were correspondents, and that meant Tours.

And Tours is a "long, long way from Tipperary. It's a long way to go."

The captain of gendarmes regarded us sternly.

"Is your car a limousine with a gray body?" he asked. We admitted that it was. "You will find it a mile farther up this road," he said. He will never know why we thanked him so extravagantly. Probably he still thinks, so anxious were we to escape, that only a car could take us away fast enough.

The chauffeur was sure he could sleep just as well outside of Rheims as in it, and on foot we returned to the city. It had now grown dark, and, as though eager to make use of the light still remaining, the salvos from the French artillery and the return fire of the Germans had quickened. Many of those we met were now panic-stricken, and, as they ran, stumbled and tripped. Women were weeping, praying aloud, and crossing themselves, and, when the shells burst, screaming in terror.

The streets and sidewalks were strewn an inch deep with the broken glass of the window-panes, and under the hurrying feet of the refugees this carpet gave out sharp, metallic echoes. With the whistling and grinding of the shells, and the crash of the falling masonry, is always associated in my mind this tinkling, musical accompaniment. Seeking a lodging for the night, and pounding on the closed doors, we walked over half the city. But no one invited us, and we were preparing to sleep in the car when we stumbled upon the Hôtel du Nord.

We found it running smoothly, and except for one man who made the beds, run by a staff composed entirely of women. That French women are capable is a bromide, but these women, under trying conditions, were especially so. They were acting as clerks, cooks, butlers, waiters, and, when their duties permitted, were industriously knitting. Their guests also were women. But they were refugees, and having no responsibility they were not capable. They sat in the pretty garden, their poodle-dogs and handbags on their knees; and each time the guns spoke, each would duck. At eight o'clock the firing had sunk to a low growl like the passing of a summer thunder-storm; and until four in the morning, when the bombardment again shook the city, there was silence. We thought what we had seen of the destruction of the cathedral required us to get our story at once on the wire; and we returned to Paris. But our judgment was at fault; we should have remained where we were. The next morning in Paris the eleven o'clock communiqué told that the cathedral was in flames, and again we started toward Rheims. It was a most difficult, and, with constantly before us the chance of arrest, a most anxious journey. A turning movement on a big scale was going forward and every foot of the way was blocked with troops. The roads could not hold them and across country they were making short cuts, the wheels of the artillery and of the motor-trucks ploughing deep furrows in the wheat-fields. We were smothered with soldiers; they clung to the running-boards of the car, were silhouetted against the sky-line, like lakes of blue they spread across the valleys, and, as though performing a gigantic snake dance, across the hills their red trousers in columns a mile long twisted and turned. Whence they came, or where they were going, we did not know. Certainly we did not ask. Into the secrets of the General Staff we had no desire to pry. We wanted only to reach Rheims and the cathedral that was in flames. For hours, purring with displeasure, the car crept through miles of infantry, cavalry, artillery, mounted gendarmes, zouaves, Turcos, ambulances, Algerian tirailleurs. In the villages they swamped the narrow streets; against the shadows of the forests their camp-fires twinkled; in the grass-gutters by the side of the road, in the fields around the stacks of grain, doubled forward or lying heavily upon their backs, they stole a moment's sleep. From a hilltop, distant six miles from Rheims, we saw the cathedral. For seven hundred years, just as for several years the Flatiron Building dominated New York City, it had dominated the countryside, and like a Rock of Gibraltar it still rose above the plain; but now, in a heavy pall, smoke rose above it; the roof was gone, part of the left tower had disappeared.

  With the goal in sight those last six miles of our journey tried our souls. We now knew that the official communiqué had told only the truth; and in pressing forward we had no more evil intent than to tell newspaper readers in the United States and Great Britain of one of the gravest crimes in history. In doing this we thought we were serving France, and by reporting the facts might possibly help in preventing further outrages. But the General Staff did not look at it in that way. To the General Staff we were potential spies; and among the thousands of soldiers we passed any one of them was justified in arresting us and sending us to Tours. In all France there were no other six miles so long.

The cathedral had been one of the most magnificent examples of early Gothic architecture. Fergusson called it "perhaps the most beautiful structure produced in the Middle Ages." It was a structure noble in its proportions, beautiful in its exquisite detail. We found the structure still standing, still noble, but the beauty was destroyed. It was like the carved statue of a saint from which some one in a drunken frenzy, with a mallet and chisel, had chopped away the features. The west façade had held five hundred and thirty statues; they were figures of the Virgin, saints, confessors, martyrs, apostles, angels. They were all mutilated, chipped, battered, dismembered. Where the day before pieces of the precious glass were missing, now whole windows, glass, lead, sash, and frame of carved stone had been torn out, and in the wall was a ragged hole. We picked our way among the broken arms, hands, wings, halos of statues that for hundreds of years, to the glory of God, had faced the elements; our feet trod upon bits of glass more beautiful than jewels. What the shells had failed to batter down, the heat of the fire, started by the shells, had destroyed. With your hands you could crumble a statue into powder; when we walked on the upper galleries above the flying buttresses, and a piece of masonry seemed unsafe, a kick would send it crashing into the street below.

The origin of the fire is now well known. Lit by a shell, it started among the scaffolding that surrounded the left tower. From the scaffolding it spread to the arched roof of oak and lead that surmounted the lower curved roof of stone. The sparks and the molten lead fell on the straw in the nave where lay the wounded.

The Abbé Chinot, a young, athletic, manly priest, and the venerable Archbishop Landreux called for volunteers, and aided by the Red Cross nurses and doctors dragged the unhappy wounded out of the burning building and through the north door. There a new danger threatened them. They were confronted by a mob. Maddened by the sight of their beloved church in flames, by the bombardment of their homes, by the death from the shells of five hundred of their townsmen, the gray uniforms drove the people of Rheims to a frenzy. They called for the death of the barbarians. What followed cannot be too often told. The aged archbishop and the young Abbé Chinot placed themselves between the mob and the wounded. With splendid indignation, with perfect courage, they faced the raised rifles. "If you kill them," they cried, "you must first kill us." And the mob, recognizing their bravery and the self-sacrifice, permitted the wounded to be carried to a place of safety. We are told that greater love hath no man than that for another he should lay down his life. If that other be his enemy, his sacrifice leads him very near to the company of the saints. The story of the young priest and the venerable archbishop, with their cathedral burning behind them, with the Germans they hated clinging to them for safety while they protected them and, in their behalf, from their own people invited death, will always live in the records of this war and of the church. It will be told in histories and in songs, and each spring will be reproduced upon the walls of the salon. With their shells the Germans hammered the nave where Joan of Arc once stood, where the monarchs of France were crowned, and destroyed the palace of the archbishop. But the spirit of the church, which is the spirit of Christ, the shells could not destroy. The two French priests proved that. With such men to keep alive the spirit, France is consoled for the loss of carved statues and rose windows.

    The Germans say they fired on the cathedral because it was being used by the French for purposes of observation. I thought that would be their excuse, and the first question I asked the Abbé Chinot was whether he had permitted the French officers to occupy the towers. I explained why the question was important, and why the facts were important. He told me most vehemently and earnestly that at no time had any officers been permitted to make use of the church for military purposes. For two nights, to protect the non-combatants of the city from air-ships, he had permitted the soldiers to place a searchlight in the tower. But, fearing this would be construed by the Germans as a hostile act, he had ordered the searchlight removed. And it was not until five nights after it had been removed that the Germans began to bombard. Abbé Chinot pointed out that had it been the searchlight to which the Germans took exception they would have shelled the tower while the light was shining, not five days after it had disappeared. During the absence of the Archbishop Landreux at Rome the Abbé Chinot had been in complete authority. And, as a priest, he gave me his solemn assurance that without his permission and knowledge no one could have entered or left the cathedral, and that by no officer or soldier had it been occupied. The other excuse of the Germans, that the French artillery was so placed that to fire at it without striking the cathedral was impossible, is so trifling as to be insolent. The cathedral was not in the line of fire between the French battery and the German battery. It was between the two French batteries.

I was in the cathedral while the Germans were shelling it. Some of their shells burst within twenty-five yards of us, and at the exact time those shells were falling I could hear the French guns to the north and south; one, a mile from us, the other, two miles. The Germans claim they were firing at those guns. To accept that, we must believe that continuously for four days they aimed at a battery and, two miles from it, hit the cathedral of Rheims.

[NOTE.—While returning from Rheims Mr. Davis and his fellow correspondents were arrested by General Asibert, and by gendarmes taken to Paris, where they were placed in the Cherche-Midi prison. Through the good offices of the American ambassador and on their giving their parole that for eight days they would not write of what they had seen along the Aisne, they were given their liberty.]

The New York Times
January 8, 1915

Wengler's "Two Shots"

Richard Harding Davis Questions Story of Officer Who Shelled Rheims Cathedral

To the Editor of The New York Times:

I have just seen a letter in THE TIMES from a correspondent in the German trenches outside of Rheims. He reports a statement made to him by Lieut. Wengler of the heavy artillery, who claims he is the officer who shelled the cathedral, at which he fired two shots, and "only two."

Wengler says, "The French observer on the cathedral was first noticed on Sept. 13 . . . the fellow continued 'on the job' quite shamelessly until the 18th, when I aimed two shots at the cathedral and only two. No more were needed to dislodge him. One from a 15-centimeter howitzer struck the top of the 'observation tower,' the other, from a 21-centimeter mortar, hit the roof and set it on fire. I wanted to dislodge the observer with the least possible damage to the fine old cathedral . . . the French also had a battery placed about 100 yards from the cathedral."

Editorially THE TIMES says such a statement may prove of "value as evidence." May I also, as evidence, tell what I saw? I arrived at the cathedral of 3 o'clock on the afternoon of the day Lieut. Wengler says he fired two shells, one of which hit the observation tower and one of which set fire to the roof. Up to the hour of 3 howitzers shells had passed through the southern wall of the cathedral, killing two of the German wounded inside, had wrecked the Grand Hotel opposite the cathedral, knocked down four houses immediately facing it, and in a dozen places torn up immense holes in the cathedral square. Twenty-four hours after Lieut. Wengler claims he ceased firing, shells set fire to the roof and utterly wrecked the chapel of the cathedral and the archbishop's palace, which is joined to the cathedral by a yard no wider than Fifth Avenue, and in the direction of the German guns the two shells fired by Lieut. Wengler had already wrecked all that part of the city surrounding the cathedral for a quarter of a mile.

To get an idea of the destruction, suppose St. Patrick's Cathedral, on Fifth Avenue, to be the Rheims Cathedral; the Union Club and the Vanderbilt houses the chapel and archbishop's palace; and all the buildings running north from St. Patrick's Cathedral to Central Park and east and west to Madison Avenue and Sixth Avenue, that part of Rheims that was utterly wrecked. That gives you some idea of the effectiveness of Lieut. Wengler's fire.

"Father," he says, "I cannot tell a lie. I did it with only two shells!"

The statement of Lieut. Wengler that the French placed a battery a hundred yards from the cathedral also is interesting. The cathedral stands in a maze of twisting narrow lanes. From no spot within a quarter of a mile of it could you drive a golf ball without smashing a window a hundred feet distant. To place a battery of artillery a hundred yards from the Rheims Cathedral with the intent of firing upon the German position would be like placing a battery in Wall Street with the idea of shelling Germans in the Bronx. Before your shells reached the Bronx you first would have to destroy all of northern New York.

Wengler says the only shells aimed at the cathedral were fired by him on the 18th, and that after that date neither he nor any other officer fired a shot. On the 22nd I was in the cathedral. It was then being shelled. I was with the Abbe Chinot, Gerald Morgan of this city, Capt. Granville Fortescue of Washington, and on the steps of the cathedral was Robert Bacon, our ex-Ambassador to France. The "evidence" of Lieut. Wengler is a question of veracity. It lies between him and these gentlemen. I am content to let it go at that.

The New York Times
July 11, 1915

An Insult to War

Miss Addams Would Strip the Dead of Honor and Courage

Mount Kisco, N.Y., July 11, 1915
To the Editor of The New York Times:

  On Friday night at Carnegie Hall Miss Jane Addams stated that in the present war, in order to get soldiers to charge with the bayonet, all nations are forced first to make them drunk. I quote from THE TIMES report:

  In Germany they have a regular formula for it [she said]. In England they use rum and the French resort to absinthe. In other words, therefore, in the terrible bayonet charges they speak of with dread, the men must be doped before they start.

  In this war the French or English soldier who has been killed in a bayonet charge gave his life to protect his home and country. For his supreme exit he had prepared himself by months of discipline. Through the winter in the trenches he has endured shells, disease, snow, and ice. For months he has been separated from his wife, children, friends—all those he most loved. When the order to charge came it was for them he gave his life, that against those who destroyed Belgium they might preserve their home, might live to enjoy peace.
  Miss Addams denies him the credit of his sacrifice. She strips him of honor and courage. She tells his children, "Your father did not die for France, or for England, or for you; he died because he was drunk."

In my opinion, since the war began, no statement has been so unworthy or so untrue and ridiculous. The contempt it shows for the memory of the dead is appalling; the credulity and ignorance it displays are inconceivable.

Miss Addams does not know that even from France they have banished absinthe. If she doubts that in this France has succeeded let her ask for it. I asked for it, and each maitre d'hotel treated me as though I had proposed we should assassinate General Joffre.

If Miss Addams does know that the French government has banished absinthe, then she is accusing it of openly receiving the congratulations of the world for destroying the drug while secretly using it to make fiends of the army. If what Miss Addams states is true, then the French government is rotten, French officers deserve only court-martial, and French soldiers are cowards.

If we are to believe her, the Canadians at Ypres, the Australians in the Dardanelles, the English and French on the Aisne made no supreme sacrifice, but were killed in a drunken brawl.

Miss Addams desires peace. So does every one else. But she will not attain peace by misrepresentation. I have seen more of this war and other wars than Miss Addams, and I know all war to be wicked, wasteful, and unintelligent, and where Miss Addams can furnish one argument in favor of peace I will furnish a hundred. But against this insult, flung by a complacent and self-satisfied woman at men who gave their lives for men, I protest. And I believe that with me are all those women and men who respect courage and honor.

New York Times
November 6, 1915

Poincaré Thanks America for Help

Good-Will and Appreciation for Sympathy Are Voiced by French President

Lauds Our Hospital Work

In Cordial Phrases He Expresses the Gratitude of All His People to Americans

PARIS, Nov. 5.—This morning President Poincaré gave me permission to convey through *The New York Times* a message to the American people.

It is a message of good will. It recognizes and appreciates the sympathy shown to France in her present fight for liberty and civilization by those Americans who remember that when we fought for our liberty France was not neutral but sent us Lafayette and Rochambeau, ships, and soldiers. It is a message of thanks from the distinguished president of the French Republic to those Americans, who not being neutral find it easier to be grateful.

It was my good fortune to be presented by Paul Benazet, a close personal friend of the president and both an officer of the army and a deputy. As a deputy before the war he helped largely in passing the bills that called for three years of military service and for heavier artillery. As an officer he won the Legion of Honor and the Cross of War. Besides being a brilliant writer, M. Benazet also is an accomplished linguist, and as President Poincaré does not express himself readily in English and as my French is better suited to restaurants than palaces, he acted as our interpreter.

The arrival of important visitors, M. Cambon, the former ambassador to the United States, and the new prime minister, M. Briand, delayed our reception, and while we waited we were escorted through the official rooms of the Elysee. It was a half hour of most fascinating interest, not only because the vast salons were filled with what in art is most beautiful, but because we were brought back to the ghosts of other days.

What we actually saw were the best of Gobelin tapestries, the best of Sevres china, the best of mural paintings. We walked on silken carpets, bearing the fleur de lys of Henry II. We sat on sofas of embroidery as fine as an engraving and as rich in color as a painting by Morland.

The bright October sunshine illuminated the ormulu, the brass of the First Empire, gilt eagles, crowns, cupids, and the only letter of the alphabet that always suggests one name.

Those whom we brought back to the rooms in which once they lived, planned, and plotted, were the ghosts of Mme. de Pompadour, Louis Quinze, Murat, Napoleon I, and Napoleon III. We could imagine the first emperor standing with his hands clasped behind him in front of the marble fireplace, his figure reflected in the full length mirrors, his features in the gold looking down at him from the walls and ceilings. We intruded even into the little room opening on the rose garden, where for hours he would pace the floor.

But perhaps what was of greatest interest was the remarkable adjustment of these surroundings, royal and imperial, to the simple and dignified needs of a republic.

France is a military nation and at war, but the evidences of militarism were entirely absent. Our own White House is not more barren of uniforms, our own president from guards of honor. One got the impression that he was entering the house of a private gentleman, a gentleman of great taste and a great nation.

We passed at last through four rooms, in which were the secretaries of the president, and as we passed the major domo spoke our names and the different gentlemen half rose and bowed. It was all so quiet, so calm, so free from telephones and typewriters that you felt that by mistake you had been ushered into the library of a student or a cabinet minister.

Then in the fourth room was the president. Without this room we were presented to M. Sainsere, the personal secretary of the president, and without further ceremony M. Benazet opened the door and in the smallest room of all introduced me to M. Poincaré. His portraits have rendered his features familiar, but they do not give sufficiently the impression I received of kindness, firmness, and great dignity.

He returned to his desk and spoke in a low voice of peculiar charm. As though the better to have the stranger understand, he spoke slowly, selecting his words.

"I have a great admiration," he said, "for the effectiveness with which Americans have shown their sympathy with France. They have sent doctors, nurses, and volunteers to drive the ambulances to carry the wounded. I have visited the hospitals at Neuilly and other places. They are admirable. The one at Neuilly was formerly a college, but with ingenuity they have converted it into a hospital, most complete and most valuable.

"The American colony in Paris has shown a friendship that we greatly appreciate. Your ambassador I have met several times. Our relations are most pleasant, most sympathetic."

I asked if I might repeat what he had said. The president gave his assent and after a pause, as though now he was to be quoted and wished to emphasize what he had said, continued:

"My wife, who distributes articles of comfort, sent to the wounded and to families in need, tells me that Americans are among the most generous contributors Many articles come anonymously—money, clothing, layettes for the babies and Lafayette kits for the soldiers. We recognize and appreciate the manner in which, while preserving a strict neutrality, your countrymen and women have shown their sympathy."

The president rose, and on leaving I presented a letter for him from ex-President Roosevelt. It was explained that this was the second for him I had had from Colonel Roosevelt, but that when a prisoner of the Germans I had judged it wise to swallow the first one, and that I had requested Colonel Roosevelt to write the second one on thin paper.

The president smiled and passed the letter critically between his thumb and forefinger. "This one," he said, "is quite digestible."

Then he gave me a message to Colonel Roosevelt and with the unconsciousness of real courtesy himself opened the door for us.

I carried away the impression of a kind and distinguished gentleman who, in the midst of the greatest crisis in history, could find time to dictate a message of appreciation to a correspondent guiltily conscious that he had wasted the precious moments of a great officer, but also through the pleasure he had received unrepentant.

The New York Times
November 16, 1915

'War As Usual' Motto of France

Soldier and Peasant Alike in Their Cheery Acceptance of the Situation

New Type in The Trenches

Mud-Caked Cavemen Unrecognizable as the French Soldiers of the Boulevards

Soldier and Plowman, Too

The Bearded "Poilu" Fights With One Hand and Tills The Soil With The Other

Paris, Nov. 15 – In England it is "Business as usual"; in France it is "War as usual." The English tradesman can assure his customers that with such an "old established" firm as his not even war can interfere; but France, with war actually on her soil, has gone further and has accepted war as part of her daily life. She has not merely swallowed, but digested it. It is like the line in Pinero's play, where one woman says she cannot go to the opera because of her neuralgia.

Her friend replies: "You can have your neuralgia in my box just as well as anywhere else." In that spirit France has accepted the war. The neuralgia may hurt, but she does not take to her bed and groan; she smiles cheerfully and courageously and goes about her duties – even sits in her box at the opera.

Highlanders Excite No Curiosity

As we approached the front – which now is a French word – this was even more evident than in Paris, where signs of war are all but invisible. Outside of Amiens we met a regiment of Scots with the pipes playing and the cold rain splashing their bare legs. To watch them pass we leaned from the car window. That we should be interested seemed to surprise them; no one else was interested. A year ago when they passed it was "roses, roses all the way" – or at least cigarettes, chocolate, and red wine. Now, in spite of the skirling bagpipes, no one turned his head. To the French they had become a part of the landscape.

A year ago the roads at every two hundred yards were barricaded. It was a continual hurdle race. Now, except at distances of four or five miles, the barricades have disappeared. One side of the road is reserved for troops, the other for moving vehicles. Those vehicles we met – for the most part two wheeled hooded carts – no longer contained peasants with their belongings flying from dismantled villages. Instead, they carried garden truck, pigs, or calves on the way to market. On the driver's seat the peasant whistled cheerily and cracked his whip. The long lines of London buses that last year advertised soap, mustard, milk and music balls, and which now are a decorous gray; the ambulances, the great guns drawn by motor trucks with caterpillar wheels, no longer surprise him.

English Now "Paying Guests"

The English ally has ceased to be a stranger and is a paying guest in the towns and villages of Artois. The shop windows are dressed chiefly for him. The names of the towns are Flemish; the names of the streets are Flemish; the names over the shops are Flemish; but the goods for sale are marmalade, tinned kippers, *The Daily Mail*, and the Pink Un.

"Is it your people who are selling those things?" I asked an English officer.

The question amused him.

"Our people won't think of it until the war is over," he said, but the French are different.

"They are capable, adaptable, and obliging. If our men ask these shopkeepers for anything they haven't got they don't say: 'We don't keep it'; they get him to write down what it is he wants, and they send for it."

It is the better way. The Frenchman does not say: "War is ruining me"; he makes the war help to support him, and at the same time gives comfort to his ally.

A year ago in the villages the old men stood in disconsolate groups with their hands in their pockets. Now they are briskly at work. They are working in the fields, in the vegetable gardens, helping the Territorials mend the roads. On every side of them were the evidences of war – in the fields abandoned trenches, barbed wire entanglement, shelters for fodder and ammunition, hangars for repairing aeroplanes, vast slaughter houses, parks of artillery; and on the roads endless lines of lorries, hooded ambulances, marching soldiers.

To us those were of vivid interest, but to the French peasant they are in the routine of his existence. After a year of it war neither greatly distresses nor greatly interests him. With one hand he fights; with the other he plows.

The First Sign of War

We had made a bet as to which would see the first sign of real war, and the sign of it that won and that gave general satisfaction, even to the man who lost, was a group of German soldiers sweeping the streets of St. Pol. They were guarded only by one of their own number, and they looked fat, sleek, and contented. When, on our return from the trenches, we saw them again, we knew they were to be greatly envied. Between standing waist high in mud in a trench and being drowned in it, buried in it, blown up or asphyxiated, the post of crossing sweeper is one to be desired.

The next sign of war was more thrilling. It was a race between a French aeroplane and German shrapnel. To us the bursting shells looked like five little cotton balls. Since this war began shrapnel, when it bursts, has invariably been compared to balls of cotton, and as that is exactly what it looks like, it is again so described. The balls of cotton did not seem to rise from the earth, but to pop suddenly out of the sky.

A moment later five more cotton balls popped out of the sky. They were much nearer the aeroplane. Others followed, leaping after it like the spray of succeeding waves. But the aeroplane steadily and swiftly conveyed itself out of range and out of our sight.

Fields Scarred with Trenches

To say where the trenches began and where they ended is difficult. We were passing through land that had been retrieved from the enemy. It had been fought for inch by inch, foot by foot. To win it back thousands of lives had been thrown like dice upon a table. There were vast stretches of mud, of fields once cultivated but now scarred with pits, trenches, rusty barbed wires.

The roads were rivers of clay. They were lined with dugouts, cellars, and caves. The burrows in the earth were supported by beams and suggested a shaft in a disused mine. They looked like the tunnels to coal pits. They were inhabited by a race of French unknown to the boulevards--men bearded, deeply tanned, and caked with clay.

Their uniforms were like those of football players on a rainy day at the end of the second half. We were entering what had been the village of Ablain, and before us rose the famous heights of Mont de Lorette. To scale these heights seemed a feat as incredible as scaling our Palisades or the sheer cliff of Gibraltar. But they had been scaled, and the side toward us was crawling with French soldiers, climbing to the trenches, descending from the trenches, carrying to the trenches food, ammunition, and fuel for the fires.

Mud, Nothing But Mud

A cold rain was falling and had turned the streets of Ablain and all the roads leading to it into swamps. In these were islands of bricks and lakes of water of the solidity and color of melted chocolate. Whatever you touched clung to you. It was a land of mud, clay, liquid earth. A cold wind whipped the rain against your face and chilled you to the bone. All you saw depressed and chilled your spirit.

To the "poilus" who, in the face of such desolation, joked and laughed with the civilians, you felt you owed an apology, for your automobile was waiting to whisk you back to a warm dinner, electric lights, red wine, and a dry bed. The men we met were cave men. When night came they would sleep in a hole in the hill fit for a mud turtle or a muskrat.

They moved in streets of clay two feet across. They were as far removed from civilization as in the past they have known it, as though they had been cast adrift upon an island of liquid mud. Wherever they looked was desolation, ruins and broken walls, jumbles of bricks, tunnels in mud, caves in mud, graves in mud.

Nothing Human About This Front

In other wars the "front" was something almost human. It advanced or wavered and withdrew at a single bugle call. It was electrified in no fixed place, but, like a wave, it enveloped a hill, or with galloping horses and cheering men overwhelmed a valley. In comparison this trench work did not suggest war. Rather it reminded you of a mining camp during the spring freshet. And for all the attention the cave men paid to them, the reports of their "seventy-fives" and the "Jack Johnsons" of the enemy bursting on Mont de Lorette might have come from miners blasting rock.

What we saw of these cave dwellers was only a few feet of a moat that for 300 miles is thrown across France like a miniature canal. Where we stood we could see of the 300 miles only mud walls, so close that we brushed one with each elbow. By looking up we could see the black lead of the sky. Ahead of us the trench twisted, and an arrow pointed to a first-aid dressing station. Behind us was the winding entrance to a shelter deep in the earth, reinforced by cement and corrugated iron and lit by a candle.

From a trench that was all we could see of this war, and it is all that the millions of fighting men can see of it – wet walls of clay as narrow as a grave, an arrow pointing to a hospital, earthen steps leading to a shelter from sudden death, and overhead the rain-soaked sky, and perhaps a great bird at which the enemy is shooting snowballs.

The New York Times
December 9, 1915

Allies in Serbia Fighting in the Clouds; Regard the Intense Cold as Their Worst Foe

SALONIKI, Dec. 4, (via Paris, Dec. 8.)—In the last two days I have been permitted to skirt the fourteen miles of French and about twelve miles of the English front in a visit so brief it is possible only to receive an impression of limitless snow-clad mountains, not in ranges but confused and interlocking, each apparently concealing a battery of artillery and each enfilading the other. It is a winter war, a war in the clouds, a war waged in the form of skylines, the horizons of which are faintly outlined and in which only artillery combats are possible.

Starting from the English base, I circled, crossing in a northeasterly direction into Serbia. The sides of the hills are dug in, like open-faced workings of mines, not against shells but the cold, the officers and men said. Though the warmest clothing is issued to them, it is no protection against this kind of cold, which is damp and penetrating. In the hospital tents and ambulances I saw a few wounded.

Leaving the western end of the English front, I entered Bulgarian territory, and from a trench position saw fifty miles of mountains with no signs of human occupation. The slopes were barren of trees. They were covered only by snow, low bushes of scrub pine, mistletoe, and rocks, and their peaks were hidden in the clouds, through which, like lightning, came the flashes of guns. At the time of my visit the French positions were being so accurately shelled that our hosts made us withdraw.

The next morning the artillery duel we saw begun ended in favor of the French, who occupied the Bulgarian position. During the last three weeks in this sector the French have been advancing, all counterattacks being repulsed.

The spirit of all the allied troops is splendid. They complain only of the cold, which is increased by lack of firewood on the hills, which are barren of woods. In spite of the condition of the roads the transport service of both forces in supplying ammunition is admirably efficient.

The New York Times
December 11, 1915

Allies at Saloniki Preparing to Stay; Many Serbian Soldiers Joining French Camp

SALONIKI, Dec. 9.—Here it is difficult to understand the discussion in the London and Paris newspapers concerning the withdrawal of the allied force from the Balkans. Evidence before the eyes of those in Saloniki is entirely opposed to such a movement.

While in Parliament and the Chamber of Deputies politicians may debate the retirement of the armies, England and France apparently are making every preparation to remain. That the line of active operation may be brought nearer to Saloniki to prevent cutting of the railroads is possible. In fact, in the last two days such a withdrawal from the Bulgarian and Serbian boundaries has gradually taken place. But of the evacuation of the territory from the boundaries to the coast there is no evidence.

On the contrary, reinforcements of British troops are arriving daily and the French are importing large numbers, and are making ready to set up wooden barracks each capable of holding 200 men. Also along the waterfront they are building storehouses of brick and stone. At the French camp in the suburbs of Saloniki when I visited it today I found thousands of soldiers actively engaged in laying stone roads, repairing bridges, and erecting new ones. There is every evidence of an intention to make this the base until the advance in the spring.

A battalion of Serbians 700 strong has arrived at the French camp. In size and physique they are splendid specimens of fighting men. They are now road-building. Each day refugees of the Serbian Army add to their number.

The New York Times
December 12, 1915

Arras, The Unburied City

Arras, Nov. 11, 1915.

In northern France there are many buried towns and villages. They are buried in their own cellars. Arras is still uninterred. She is the corpse of a city that waits for burial, and day by day the German shells are trying to dig her grave. They were at it yesterday when we visited Arras, and this morning they will be hammering her again.

Seven centuries before this war Arras was famous for her tapestries, so famous that in England a tapestry was called an arras. Now she has given her name to a battle—to different battles—that began with the great bombardment of October a year ago, and each day since then have continued. On one single day, June 26, the Germans threw into the city shells in all sizes, from three to sixteen inches, and to the number of 10,000. That was about one for each house.

This bombardment drove 2,700 inhabitants into exile, of whom 1,200 have now returned. The army feeds them, and in response they have opened shops that the shells have not already opened, and supply the soldiers with tobacco, postcards, fruit and vegetables from those gardens not hidden under bricks and cement. In the deserted city these civilians form an inconspicuous element. You can walk for great distances and see none of them. When they do appear in the empty streets they are like ghosts. Every day the shells change one or two of them into real ghosts. But the others still stay on. With the dogs nosing among the fallen bricks, and the pigeons on the ruins of the cathedral, they know no other home.

As we entered Arras the silence fell like a sudden change of temperature. Every corner seemed to threaten an ambush. Our voices echoed so loudly that unconsciously we spoke in lower tones. The tap of the captain's walking stick resounded like the blow of a hammer. The emptiness and stillness was like that of a vast cemetery, and the grass that has grown through the paving stones deadened the sound of our steps, This silence was broken only by the barking of the French seventy-fives, in parts of the city hidden to us, the boom of the German guns in answer, and from overhead by the aeroplanes. In the absolute stillness the whirl of their engines came to us with the steady vibrations of a loom.

Under our feet were shell holes that had been recently filled and covered over with bricks and fresh earth. It was like walking upon newly made graves. On either side were cellars into which the houses had dumped themselves, or, still balancing above them, were walls prettily papered, hung with engravings, paintings, mirrors, quite intact. These walls were roofless and defenseless against the rain and snow. Other houses were like those toy ones built for children, with the front open. They showed a bed with pillows, shelves supporting candles, books, a washstand with basin and pitcher, a piano, and a reading lamp.

In one house four stories had been torn away, leaving only the attic sheltered by the peaked roof. To that height no one could climb, and exposed to view were the collection of trunks and boxes familiar to all attics. As a warning against rough handling, one of these, a woman's hatbox, had been marked "fragile." Secure and serene, it smiled down sixty feet upon the mass of iron and bricks it had survived.

The pure deviltry of a shell no one can explain. Nor why it spares a looking-glass and wrecks a wall that has been standing since the twelfth century. It loves a shining mark. To what is most beautiful it is most cruel. The Hotel de Ville, which was counted among the most presentable in the north of France, and which once rose in seven arches in the style of the Renaissance, the shells marked for their own. And all the houses approaching it from the German side they destroyed. Not even those who once lived in them could say where they stood. There is left only a mess of bricks, tiles, and plaster.

We visited what had been the headquarters of General de Wignacourt. They were in the garden of a house that opened upon one of the principal thoroughfares, and the floor level was twelve feet under the level of the flower beds.

Here, secure from falling walls and explosive shells, the general, by telephone, directed his attack. The place was as dry, as clean, and as compact as the admiral's quarters on a ship of war. The switchboard was connected with batteries buried from sight in every part of the buried city, and in an adjoining room a soldier cook was preparing a most appetizing luncheon. Above us was three yards of cement, rafters and earth, and crowning them grass and flowers. When the owner of the house returns he will find this addition to his residence an excellent refuge from burglars or creditors.

We lunched in a charming house where the table was spread in the front hall. The bed of the officer temporarily occupying the house also was spread in the hall, and we were curious to know, but too proud to ask, why he limited himself to such narrow quarters. Our captain rewarded our reticence. He threw back the heavy curtain that concealed the rest of the house and showed us that the remainder had been deftly removed by a shell.

The owner of the house had run away, but before he went, fearing the Germans might enter Arras and take his money, he had withdrawn it and hid it in the garden. The money amounted to $2,500. He placed it in a lead box, soldered up the opening, and buried the box under a tree. Then he went away and carelessly forgot which tree. During a lull in the bombardment he returned, and until 2 in the morning dug frantically for his buried treasure. The soldier who guarded the house told me the difference in the way the soldiers dig a trench, and the way our absent host dug for his lost money was greatly marked. I found the leaden box cast aside in the dog kennel. It was the exact size of a suitcase. As none of us knows when he may not have to bury $2,500 hurriedly, it is a fact worth remembering. Any ordinary suitcase will do. The soldier and I examined the leaden box carefully. But the owner had not overlooked anything.

When we reached the ruins of the cathedral we did not need darkness and falling rain to further depress us or to make the scene more desolate. One lacking in all reverence would have been shocked. The wanton waste, the senseless brutality in such destruction would have moved a statue. Walls as thick as the ramparts of a fort had been blown into powdered chalk; there were great breaches in them through which you could drive an omnibus. In one place the stone roof and supporting arches had fallen, and upon the floor, where for 200 years the people of Arras had knelt in prayer, was a mighty barricade of stone blocks, twisted candelabra, broken praying chairs, town vestments, and shattered glass. Exposed to the elements, the chapels were open to the sky. The rain fell on sacred emblems of the Holy Family, the saints and apostles.

The destruction is too great for present repair. They can fill the excavations in the streets, and board up the shattered show windows. But the cathedral is too vast, the destruction of it too nearly complete. The sacrilege must stand. Until the war is over, until Arras is free from shells, the ruins must remain uncared for and uncovered.

The New York Times
December 13, 1915

Americans Escape Safely from Gievgeli

Mme. Grouitch Reaches Saloniki With 38 Orphans—Why Allies are Retreating

SALONIKI, Dec. 11.—There seems to be no longer any doubt that Gievgeli was evacuated early Friday by the French and Serbian forces. The Serbian inhabitants had already fled. On account of the bombardment even the Bulgarian residents moved out. The director of the Post Office, who arrived here this morning by horseback, says he was the last to leave the city, which was being bombarded.

He says shells set fire to the former American Hospital operated by Dr. James Donnelly, and which, after his death, was taken over by the French for the French and Serbian wounded, all of whom were safely removed. The railroad station was also destroyed.

Mme. Mabel Grouitch, the Serbian-American in charge of the Frothingham unit, with her assistant, Elva Reed La Grane of Oregon, left Gievgeli on the 9th, bringing safely here in a freight car thirty-eight Serbian orphans. These women are doing splendid work. The orphanage, which is supported by Mr. Frothingham of Baltimore, was originally at Nish. When driven from there the staff took refuge at Gievgeli. When your correspondent visited Gievgeli last week these women were managing restaurants, with the profits of which they supported the orphans. Lady Scott's unit of five nurses, who are Scotch, also escaped safely. No Americans or English remain in Gievgeli.

Refugees are now crowding into Saloniki on mattresses in carts, carrying their pitiful possessions in kerchiefs and baskets. It is a picture of this war that has been made familiar, but that these refugees are forerunners of a Bulgarian advance upon Saloniki does not follow. But Gievgeli is so near the border that if the Bulgarians mean to halt there or fight on Greek soil the next few hours should decide.

It is now possible to give in more detail an explanation of the withdrawal of the French and British to their second line of defense. To understand this withdrawal find on the map Krivolak, the former French advanced position, and follow the railroad and River Vardar southeast to Gradec, the present first French line.

The cause of this retreat is the inability to hold Monastir, and their withdrawal west is leaving a gap in the former line of the Serbians, French and British. The enemy is now south and west of the French, and their left flank is exposed.

On Dec. 3, finding the advanced position at Krivolak threatened by four divisions—100,000 men—General Sarrall began the withdrawal, sending south by rail without loss all ammunition and stores. He destroyed the tunnel at Krivolak and all the bridges across the Vardar and on his left at the Cerna River. The fighting was heavy at Prevedo and Biserence, but the French losses were small. He withdrew slowly twenty miles in one week and established his advanced position at Demir-Kapu, with his first line at Gradec. The British also withdrew from their first line to their second line of defense. Kosturino, in the Bojimia Valley, and the important Hill 516 are also believed to be lost.

Demir-Kapu, meaning the Gate of Iron, is the entrance to a beautiful and celebrated valley. Starting at Demir-Kapu and ending two kilometers north of Gradec, it rises on either side of the Vardar River and a railroad line, in places less than 300 yards wide, formed by sheer hills, rocky, treeless and exposed. For five miles along the crests of this narrow pass the French artillery is now placed.

Last week your correspondent visited Gradec, then occupied only by two companies of infantry. All the inhabitants had fled. It was a mud village which last year had been practically destroyed. Until now it had been known chiefly for its ancient church, richly decorated with paintings on the walls inside and without. At the request of the commanding officer, Merse, I took many photographs to send to his wife to show here where he expected to spend the winter.

Hill 516 is the most important position, as it commands the valley of the Vardar. Last week, while I was visiting this hill, the Bulgarian fire was already so accurate that shells fell within 100 to 40 feet of us. If it is true that it is now occupied by the Bulgarians, this explains the withdrawal of the British line, which on that day, Dec. 3, was shelled from a hill a quarter of a mile distant and below us.

This afternoon a Greek military mission from Athens and General Sarrall discussed the question what course will be followed should the Bulgars cross the Greek border.

[Mr. Davis's dispatch is dated on Saturday. Advices received in London that morning from Reuter's Saloniki correspondent announced that there was good authority for the statement that Gievgeli had been occupied by the Germans the previous day. Subsequent dispatches stated that the announcement was premature and at latest accounts the Allies still held the town.]

The New York Times
December 15, 1915

Allies' Casualties in Retreat Given as 1,700; Bulgars Hold American Woman at Monastir

SALONIKI, Dec. 13.—This morning's local papers are of the opinion that, while the Bulgars will not cross the border, the Germans and Austrians will make a direct drive toward Saloniki. Many inhabitants of the richer class have applied for passports. Some, more timid, have already packed their bags.

Yesterday British transports disembarked reinforcements of artillery and infantry. Owing to this port being neutral, a peculiar condition exists which makes it possible for Turkish and German spies freely to watch these landings. Every horse, man, and box of ammunition is counted, and the information forwarded to the enemy, now not more than forty miles distant.

This morning the train to Doiran was denied to civilians, but passenger traffic probably will be resumed as soon as the reinforcements have been sent to the front.

At military headquarters it is stated that the losses during the retreat from Krivolak were for the French 700 and for the British, who were in the direct line of attack, 1,000. The military situation is regarded with confidence and equanimity. Evidence of this is that General Sarrall has invited the correspondents to visit the front, which does not look as though an immediate withdrawal was considered probable.

Walter Farwell of Chicago and Texas, brother of Mrs Chatfield Taylor and Mrs. Reginald de Koven, left here three days ago to bring his wife out of Monastir, where she went as correspondent of a Chicago paper. Since the city has been occupied no word has been received from her.

Tonight Mr. Farwell arrived here, turned back by the Bulgars, ten miles from Monastir, in spite of the fact that he was accompanied by Mr. Loughlin, agent of the American Red Cross Sanitary Corps, and was bearing credentials from our consul. Mr. Farwell was held one day while his request was telegraphed to Sofia, during which period he assisted in burying Serbian dead. His request that he be permitted to send a note to his wife was refused.

He will not attempt to get her out of Sofia.

The New York Times
December 31, 1915

Luring Teutons On To Saloniki

French Generals Who Fought Before Paris Use Same Tactics in Greece

Allies Hold Strong Lines And Intend to Stick, If Only to Repay Russia's Tannenburg Sacrifice

Paris, Dec. 30. – The same team that, to put it politely, drew the enemy after them to the gates of Paris, have been drawing the same enemy after them to Saloniki. That they will throw him back from Saloniki, as they threw him back from Paris, is assured.

General Sarrail, who was one of those who commanded in front of Paris, commands the Allies in Greece, and General Castelnau, who also commanded at the battle of the Marne and is now Chief of Staff of General Joffre, has just visited Saloniki. He was sent to "go, look, and see." He reports that the position, now held by the Allies, is impregnable.

The perimeter, held by the Allies, is fifty miles in length, from the Vardar River on the west to the Gulf or Orphanos on the east. There are three lines of defence. To assist the first two on the east are Lakes Beshik and Langaza and on the west is the Vardar River. Should the enemy penetrate the first lines they will be confronted ten miles from Saloniki by a natural barrier of hills. Should they surmount these hills the allied warships in the harbor can sweep them off those hills as a firehose rips the shingles off a roof.

The man who pretends to understand the situation in Saloniki is of the same mental caliber as one who understands a system for beating the game at Monte Carlo. But there are certain rumors as to what the situation may become that can be eliminated. First, Greece will not turn against the Allies. Second, the Allies will not withdraw from Saloniki. They now are agreed that it is better to resist and attack or stand a siege, even if they lose 200,000 men, than to withdraw without a fight.

Easy Field for Spies to Work

The Government here believes that had the Government it overthrew in October sent troops to aid the Serbian Army four months ago this war would have been shorter by six months. The present Government is now determined. Apart from resisting the advance of the German-Austrian-Bulgarian forces the presence of 200,000 men at Saloniki will hold Rumania from any aggressive movement on Russia.

To aid the Allies Russia at Tannenberg made a sacrifice and lost 200,000 men. The French now feel bound in honor to see by keeping the armies at Saloniki that Russia is not threatened. As a member of the Government said to me today: "There is no western line or eastern line. The line of the Allies is wherever a German attacks. France went to the Balkans to help Serbia. She went too late, which is not the fault of the present Government. But there remains to keep the Germans from Egypt and to keep Rumania from an attack upon the flank of Russia. The Allies are in Saloniki until this war is ended."

In Saloniki I saw many evidences that this is the purpose of the Allies, that both England and France are determined to hold fast. The French were building barracks of stone and brick, and erecting ready-to-set-up houses, each capable of holding 250 men. Their camp outside the city was five miles square. Following the plans of their engineers, they were building roads, draining, repairing bridges and erecting new ones.

On the 14th December, when the Greek Army evacuated Saloniki the buildings and open places, formerly occupied by them, were taken over by the British for garages, parking places, storehouses, and machine shops for auto trucks, and from the transports began disembarking thousands of men.

To Repay Russian Sacrifice

The censor would not permit me to say what numbers of men, stores, guns and ammunition were brought ashore. But it is one of the peculiarities of the situation that it's something that every German knows. Probably in no other war has a condition so remarkable existed.

A German correspondent with the German forces in Monastir claims that he has already visited Saloniki; seen everything that was to be seen in the way of preparation, even the trenches in the first lines of defense, and returned to Monastir. In this there is nothing improbable. He could have come to Saloniki also from Berlin via Constantinople for Saloniki is still a neutral port and therefore is the haven and happy hunting ground for spies.

A German spy, who watches the Allies preparing to meet his army is in no more danger than when he watches his wife cook his coffee and black his boots. Upon a Greek city of 120,000 allied troops have descended, but the local authority is still Greek.

At the base of an army there always has been martial law, countersigns, passports and passwords. But at Saloniki, any German, Austrian, Turkish or Bulgarian officer, if out of uniform, instead of being shot, can go where he likes, see what he likes, and report to his intelligence department.

From my room in the Hotel Olympos one could count guns on every battleship or torpedo boat, be it British, French, Russian, or Italian, that entered the harbor, and at a distance of a hundred yards could watch the transports unload. You could not approach your window without seeing something that even a friend should not have seen. It made one feel as if he had been reading another man's letters.

And a German did not need to look from the window. Like everyone else he was free to go down to the very landing stage and with a pencil and notebook check off the men, horses, and guns.

One Greek newspaper every morning printed just what had been brought ashore, but as it always undervalued and sneered at what it saw, it rendered valuable service. In spite of petty obstructions by local Greek officials, and in spite of spies, a great army has been landed.

In the event the fight will not be pulled off on the wharves. It will be waged along the fifty-mile front, and if the spies have reported only half of what every one was free to see, by now the Germans know what men await them.

The New York Times
January 2, 1916

Air Raiders Aimed at Allies' Warships

Seizure of the Teuton Consuls at Saloniki a Natural Reprisal

PARIS, Jan. 1.—The raid of Bulgarian and German aeroplanes over Saloniki reported in the French bulletin does not necessarily mean that an attack by troops will follow. London and Paris were raided by aircraft, but no troops have yet reached those cities.

Nor is it probable that the raid was for the purpose of observation. There is no need to send a man conspicuously in an aeroplane to count the warships in the harbor when an inconspicuous man on the wharf has for weeks been furnishing more accurate information, and when Saloniki is full of spies who are able to communicate with Doiran, Gevgheli, and Monastir.

An observer 2,000 yards in the air would be unable to tell the Central Powers anything of which they are not already informed. Their agents are on the quays, streets, and roads leading to and beyond the military camps, and even at work building roads in the camps.

The object of the raid was more likely for moral effect or to throw bombs on transports and warships. The bomb reported dropped upon a battalion of Greek soldiers was probably launched by mistake, owing to the Greek uniform being of khaki colored cloth similar to the British at a distance.

It is evident that the French squadron of aircraft were taken by surprise, and that if the raiders return they will receive a warmer welcome, as during the Serbian campaign the French aeroplanes showed splendid efficiency and furnished valuable information. This was accomplished under most unfavorable conditions of snow, fog, and treacherous cross-currents above valleys and over a terrain barren of landing places.

In arresting and removing the consuls of the enemy in reprisal for the raid, General Sarrall followed the only possible course. The consulates have been the headquarters of army and navy officers of the Central Powers, Turkey and Bulgaria, besides furnishing a clearing house for all the spies.

Saloniki is supposed to be neutral territory, but the presence of foreign consuls at the base of two armies has been a most serious menace. Their enforced departure will add to the responsibilities of the American consul in looking after their interests. Our government is represented in Saloniki by John E. Kehl, long in the service and most admirably fitted to meet the present crisis. He has been a resident of Saloniki for the last four years, during which his experience as Consul during the Italo-Turkish war, the two Balkan wars, and the present one has trained him to meet any emergency that may now arise.

When the Greeks captured Saloniki Consul Kehl was one of those sent out to meet King Constantine and arrange that the city should not be bombarded.

The position of a consul in Saloniki, owing to the former ex-territorial privileges and right to conduct trials and sentence to death, gives the post peculiar authority. In importance it outranks many legations. The consulates are all established in an imposing building, surrounded by gardens and trees, facing the harbor on Reine Olga street, and guarded by a staff of uniformed kavess.

Before I left Saloniki the consuls of the Central Powers had already sent their families to Athens and were arranging with Consul Kehl to take over their archives.

The New York Times
January 12, 1916

Allies' Grip on Food Keeps Greece Still

Country Cannot Afford to Take Any Action to Offend Nations Holding the Sea.

Situation Full of Snarls

Everybody, from Cabinet Ministers to Brigands, Ready and Eager to Explain It

ATHENS, Nov. 29, 1915.—We are not allowed to tell what the situation is here. But in spite of the censor, I am going to tell what the situation is. It is involved. That is not because no one will explain it. In Athens no one does anything else. Since arriving yesterday I have had the situation explained to me by members of the Cabinet, guides to the Acropolis, generals in the army, Teofani the cigarette king, three ministers plenipotentiary, the man from St. Louis who is over here to sell aeroplanes, the man from Cook's, and "extra people" like soldiers in cafes, brigands in petticoats, and peasants in peaked shoes with tassels. They asked me not to print their names, which was just as well, as I cannot spell them. They are written in the language that made Dr. Jowett famous. They each explained the situation differently, but all agree it is involved.

To understand it, you must go back to Helen of Troy, take a running jump from the Greek war for independence and Lord Byron to Mr. Gladstone and the Bulgarian atrocities, note the influence of the German emperor at Corfu, appreciate the intricacies of Russian diplomacy in Belgrade, the rise of Enver Pasha and the Young Turks, what Constantine said to Venizelos about giving up Kavalla, and the cablegram Prince Danilo, of

"Merry Widow" fame, sent to his cousin of Italy. By following these events the Situation is as easy to grasp as an eel that has swallowed the hook and can't digest it.

For instance, Mr. Poneropolous, the well-known contractor who sells shoes to the army, informs me the Greeks as one man want war. They are even prepared to fight for it. On the other hand, Axon Skiadas, the popular barber of the Hotel Grande Bretagne, who has just been called to the colors, assures me no patriot would again plunge the country into conflict. To Axon the thought is personally so distasteful that he says, "It makes me a headache."

Diplomats Also Disagree

The diplomats here also disagree, especially as to which of them is responsible for the failure of Greece to join the Allies. The one who is to blame for that never is the one who is talking to you. The one who is talking is always the one who, had they followed his advice, could have saved the "Situation." They did not, and now it is involved, not to say addled. One military attaché of the Allies volunteered to set the Situation before me in a few words. After explaining for two hours, he asked me to promise not to repeat what he had said. I promised. Another diplomat, who was projected into the service by the late William Jennings Bryan, said if he told all he knew about the situation "the world would burst." Those are his exact words. It would have been an event of undoubted news value, and as a news gatherer I should have coaxed his secret from him, but it seemed as though the world is in trouble enough as it is, and if it must burst I want it to burst when I am nearer home. So I switched him off to the St. Louis Convention, where he was probably more useful than he will ever be in the Balkans.

While every one is guessing, your correspondent ventures to make a guess. It is that long before this letter reaches America, Greece will be demobilized, and will remain neutral, or will have joined the Allies. Without starving to death she cannot join the Germans. Greece is non-supporting. What she eats comes in the shape of wheat from outside her borders, from the grain fields of Russia, Egypt, Bulgaria, France, and America. Last week, when Denys Cochin, the French minister to Athens, had his interview with the king, the latter became angry and said "We can get along without France's money," and Cochin said, "That is so, but you cannot get along without France's wheat."

The Allies are not going to bombard Greek ports or shell the Acropolis. They will not even blockade the ports. But their fleets—French, Italian, English—will stop all ships taking foodstuffs to Greece. They have just released seven grain ships from America that were held up at Malta, and ships carrying food to Greece have been stopped at points as far away as Gibraltar. The steamer on which we came here from Naples was held up at Messina for twenty-four hours until her cargo was overhauled. As we had nothing in the hold more health-sustaining than hides and barbed wire we were allowed to proceed.

Whatever course Greece follows, her dependence upon others for food explains her act. Today (Nov. 29) there is not enough wheat in the country to feed the people for, some say three—the most optimistic, ten—days. Should she decide to join Germany she would starve. It would be deliberate suicide. The French and Italian fleets are at Malta, less than a day distant; the English fleet is off the Gallipoli peninsula. Fifteen hours' steaming could bring it to Saloniki. Greece is especially vulnerable from the sea. She is all islands, coast towns, and seaports. The German Navy could not help her. It will not leave the Kiel Canal. The Austrian Navy cannot leave Trieste. Should Greece decide against the allies their combined warships would pick up her islands and blockade her ports. In a week she would be starving. The railroad from Bulgaria to Saloniki, over which in peace times comes much wheat from Rumania, would be closed to her. Even if the Germans and

Bulgarians succeeded in winning it to the coast, they could get no food for Greece further than that. They have no warships, and the Gulf of Saloniki is full of those of the Allies.

King's Position Difficult

The position of King Constantine is very difficult. He is strongly pro-German, and the reason for his sympathy that is given here is the same as is accepted in America. Every act of his is supposed to be inspired by his sympathies, when, in several instances, he has been actuated solely by what he thought was best for his own people. Indeed, there are many who believe if the terms upon which Greece might join the Allies had been left to the King instead of to Venizelos, Greece would now be with the Entente.

As long as when the two German cruisers escaped from Messina and were sold to Turkey, the diplomatic representatives of the Allies in the Balkans were instructed to see that Turkey and Germany did not get together, and that, as a balance of power in case of such a union, the Balkan States were kept in line. Instead of attending to this themselves, the diplomats placed this delicate job in the hands of one man. At the framing of the Treaty of London, of all the representatives from the Balkans, the one who most deeply impressed the other powers was M. Venizelos. And the task of keeping the Balkans neutral or with the Allies was left to him.

He has a dream of a Balkan "band," a union of all the Balkan principalities. It obsesses him. And to bring that dream true he was willing to make concessions which King Constantine, who considered only what was good for Greece, thought most unwise. Venizelos also was working for the good of Greece, but he was convinced it could come to her only through the union. He was willing to give Kavalla to Bulgaria in exchange for Asia Minor, from the Dardanelles to Smyrna. But the king would not consent. As a buffer against Turkey he considered Kavalla of the greatest strategic value, and he had the natural pride of a soldier in holding on to land he himself had added to his country. But in his opposition to Venizelos in this particular credit was not given him for acting in the interests of Greece, but of playing into the hands of Germany.

Another step he refused to take, which refusal the Allies attributed to his pro-German leanings, was to attack the Dardanelles. In the wars of 1912-1913 the King showed he was an able general. With his staff he had carefully considered an attack upon the Dardanelles. He submitted this plan to the Allies and was willing to aid them if they brought to the assault 400,000 men. They claim he failed them. He did fail them, but not until after they had failed him by bringing thousands of men instead of the tens of thousands he knew were needed.

The Dardanelles expedition was not required to prove the courage of the French and British. Beyond furnishing fresh evidence of that, it has been a failure. And in refusing to sacrifice the lives of his subjects the military judgment of Constantine has been vindicated. He was willing to attack Turkey through Kavalla and Thrace, because by that route he presented an armed front to Bulgaria. But, as he pointed out, if he sent his army to the Dardanelles, he left Kavalla at the mercy of his enemy. The mistrust of Bulgaria also has been justified.

But whether Constantine or Venizelos was the better friend of Greece is now ancient history and important only as a subject for discussion, It is a condition that confronts Greece. She cannot now choose whether she will follow the advice of king or prime minister. The Allies are using an argument that every goatherd can understand. When a man is hungry and only one man can feed him he may not become the ally of that man, but he will not fight him.

The New York Times
January 19, 1916

French Made Merry in Serbian Retreat

Toasted Their Allies and American Guests in Bumpers of Champagne

Fought Invisible Enemies

Big Guns Seemed to be "Attacking Fifty Miles of Landscape"—Invincibly Cheerful "Poilus"

SALONIKI, Dec. 13.—The chauffeur of an army automobile must make his way against cavalry, artillery, motor trucks, motorcycles, men marching and ambulances filled with wounded over a road torn by thousand-ton lorries and excavated by washouts and Jack Johnsons. It is therefore necessary for him to drive with care. So, he drives at sixty miles an hour and tries to scrape the mud from every wheel he meets.

In these days of his downfall the greatest danger to the life of the war correspondent is that he must move about in automobiles driven by military chauffeurs. The one who drove me from the extreme left of the English front up to Hill 516, which was the highest point of the French front, told me in peace times he drove a car to amuse himself. His idea of amusing himself was to sweep around a corner on one wheel, exclaim with horror, and throw on all the brakes with the nose of the car projecting over a precipice a hundred yards deep. He knew perfectly well the precipice was there, but he leaped at it exactly as though it were the finish line of the Vanderbilt cup race. If his idea of amusing himself was to make me sick with terror, he must have spent a thoroughly enjoyable afternoon.

The approaches to Hill 516, the base of the hill on the side hidden from the Bulgarians, and the trenches dug into it were crowded with the French. At that point of the line they greatly outnumbered the English. But it was not the elbow touch of numbers that explained their cheerfulness; it was because they knew it was expected of them. The famous scholar who wrote in our school geographies, "The French are a gay people, fond of dancing and light wines" established a tradition. And on Hill 516, although it was to keep from freezing that they danced, and though the light wines were melted snow, they still kept up that tradition and were "gay." They laughed at us in welcome, crawling out of their igloos on all fours like bears out of a cave; they laughed when we photographed them crowding to get in front of the camera when we scattered among them copies of *l'Opinion*, when up the snow-clad hillside we skidded and slipped and fell. And if we peered into the gloom of the shelters, where they crouched on the frozen ground with snow dripping from above, with shoulders pressed against walls of icy mud, they waved spoons at us and invited us to share their soup. Even the dark skinned, somber-eyed men of the desert, the tall Moors and Algerians, showed their white teeth and laughed when a "seventy-five" exploded from an unsuspicious bush and we jumped. It was like a camp of boy scouts picnicking for one day and sure the same night of a warm supper and bed. But the best these "poilus" might hope for was months of ice, snow and mud, of discomfort, colds, long marches carrying heavy burdens, the pain of frostbite and worst of all, of homesickness. They were sure of nothing, not even of the next minute. For Hill 516 was dotted with oblong rows of stones, with at one end a cross of green twigs and a soldier's cap.

Firing at Invisible Positions

The hill was the highest point of a ridge that looked down into the valley of the Vardar and of Bodjinia. Toward the Bulgarians we could see the one village of Kosturino, almost indistinguishable against the snow, and for fifty miles, even with glasses, no other signs of life. Nothing but hills, rocks, bushes and snow. When the "seventy-fives" spoke with their smart, sharp crack that always seems to say "Take that!" and to add with aristocratic insolence "And be damned to you!" one could not conceive what they were firing at. In Champagne, where the Germans were as near as a hundred to forty yards; in Artois, where they were a mile distant, but where their trench was as clearly in sight as the butts of a rifle range, you could understand. You knew that "that dark line over there" was the enemy. In other little wars you had watched the shells destroy a blockhouse, a village, or burst upon a column of men. But from Hill 516 you could see no enemy—only mountains draped in snow, silent, empty, inscrutable. It seemed ridiculous to be attacking fifty miles of landscape with tiny pills of steel. But although we could not see the Bulgars, they could see the flashes on Hill 516, and from somewhere out of the inscrutable mountains shells burst and fell. They fell very close, and, like children being sent to bed just at dessert time, our hosts hurried us out of the trenches and drove us away.

While on "516" we had been in Bulgaria; now we returned to Serbia, and were halted at the village of Valandova. There had been a ceremony there that afternoon. A general whose name we may not mention had received the Medaille Militaire. One of the French correspondents asked him in recognition of which of his victories it had been bestowed. The general possessed a snappy temper.

"The medal was given me," he said, "because I was the only general without it, and I was becoming conspicuous."

It had long been dark when we reached Strumnitza station, where we were to spend the night in a hospital tent. The tent was as big as a barn, with a stove, a cot for each, and fresh, linen sheets. All these good things belong to the men we had left on Hill 516 awake in the mud and snow. I felt like a burglar who, while the owner is away, sleeps in his bed. There was another tent with a passageway filled with medical supplies connecting it with ours. It was in darkness, and we thought it empty until someone exploring found it crowded with wounded and men with frozen legs and hands. For half an hour they had been watching us through the passageway, making no signs, certainly making no complaint. John Bass collected all our newspapers, candles, and boxes of cigarettes, which the hospital stewards distributed, and when we returned from dinner our neighbors were still wide awake and holding a smoking concert. But when in the morning the bugles woke up, we found that during the night the wounded had been spirited away and by rail transferred to the hospital ships. We should have known then that the army was in retreat. But it was all so orderly, so leisurely, that it seemed like merely a shifting from one point of the front to another.

We dined with the officers, and they certainly gave no suggestion of men contemplating retreat, for the messa hall in which dinner was served had been completed only that afternoon. It was of rough stones and cements, and the interior walls were covered with whitewash. The cement was not yet dry, and as John McCutcheon later discovered when he drew caricatures on it, neither was the whitewash. There were twenty men around the dinner table, seated on ammunition boxes and Standard Oil cans, and so close together you could use only one hand. So you gave up trying to cut your food and used the free hand solely in drinking toasts to the army, to France and the Allies; then to each ally individually. You were glad there were so many allies, for it was not Greek, but French wine of the kind that comes from Rheims. And the army was retreating. What the French Army offers its guests when it is advancing it is difficult to imagine.

A Black Prince as a Waiter

We were waited upon by an enormous negro from Senegal with a fez as tall as a giant firecracker. Waiting single-handed on twenty men is a serious matter. And because the officers laughed when he served the soup in a tin basin used for washing dishes, his feelings were hurt. It was explained that "Chocolat" in his own country was a prince, and that, unless treated with tact, he might get the idea that waiting on a table is not a royal prerogative. One of the officers was a genius at writing impromptu verses. During one course he would write them and while Chocolat was collecting the plates would sing them. Then, by the light of a candle on the back of a scrap of paper, he would write another and sing that. He was rivaled in entertaining us by the officers who told anecdotes of war fronts from the Marne to Smyrna, who proposed toasts and made speeches in response, especially by the officer who that day had received the Croix de Guerre and a wound.

I sat next to a young man who had been talking learnedly of dumdum bullets and Parisitan restaurants. They asked him to recite, and to my horror he rose. Until that moment he had been a serious young officer, talking boulevard French. In an instant he was transformed. He was a clown. To look at him was to laugh. He was an old roué, senile, pitiable, a bourgeois, an Apache, a lover, and his voice was so beautiful that each sentence sang. He used words so difficult that to avoid them even Frenchmen will cross the street. He mastered them, played with them, caressed them, sipped of them as a connoisseur sips Madeira; he tossed them into the air like radiant bubbles, or flung them at us with the rattle of a mitrailleuse. When in triumph he sat down I asked him, when not in uniform, who the devil he happened to be.

Again he was the bored young man. In a low tone, so as not to expose my ignorance to the others, he said:

"I? I am Barrielles of the Theatre Odeon."

We were receiving so much that to make no return seemed ungracious, and we insisted that John T. McCutcheon should decorate the wall of the new mess room with the caricatures that made the *Chicago Tribune* famous. Our hosts were delighted, but it was hardly fair to McCutcheon. Instead of his own choice of weapons, he was asked to prove his genius on wet whitewash with a stick of charred wood. It was like asking McLaughlin to make good on a plowed field. But in spite of the fact that the whitewash fell off in flakes, there grew upon the wall a tall, gaunt figure with gleaming eyes and teeth. Chocolat paid it the highest compliment. He gave a wild howl, and fled into the night. Then in quick succession, while the Frenchmen applauded each swift stroke, appeared the faces of the songwriter, the comedian, the wounded man, and the commanding officer. It was a real triumph, but the surprises of the evening were not at an end. McCutcheon had but just resumed his seat when the newly finished rear wall of the mess hall crashed into the room. Where had been rocks and cement was a gaping void, and a view of a garden white with snow.

While we were rescuing the songwriter from the debris McCutcehon regarded the fallen wall thoughtfully.

"They feared," he said, "I was going to decorate that wall also, and they sent Chocolat outside to push it in."

The next day we walked along the bank of the Vardar River to Gravec, about five miles north of Strumnitza station. Five miles further was Demir Kapou, the Gate of Iron, and between these two towns is a high and narrow pass, famous for its wild and magnificent beauty. Fifteen miles beyond that was Krivolak, the most advanced French position. On the hills above Gravec were many guns, but in the town itself only a few infantrymen. It was a town entirely of mud; the houses, the roads and the people were covered with it. Gravec is proud only of its church, on the walls of which in colors still rich are painted many devils with pitchforks driving the wicked ones into the flames.

One of the "poilus" put his finger on the mass of wicked ones.

"Les Boches," he explained.

Whether the devils were the French or the English he did not say, possibly because at the moment they were more driven against than driving.

A Snapshot for His Wife

Major Merse, the commanding officer, invited us to his headquarters. They were in a house of stone and mud, from which projected a wooden platform. When any one appeared upon it he had the look of being about to make a speech. The major asked us to take photographs of Gravec and send them to his wife. He wanted her to see in what sort of place he was condemned to exist during the winter. He did not wish her to think of him as sitting in front of a café on the sidewalk, and the snapshots would show her that Gravec hs no cafés, no sidewalks and no streets. But he was not condemned to spend the winter in Gravec.

Within the week great stores of ammunition and supplies began to pour into it from Krivolak, and the Gate of Iron became the advanced position, and Gravec suddenly found herself of importance as the French base. It was a short-lived fame. The Gate of Iron belied her ancient name, and, with a hundred thousand Bulgars crowding down upon her, General Sarrail wasted no lives, either French or Egnlish, but withdrew. He was outnumbered some way five to one. In any event, he was outnumbered as inevitably as three of a kind beat two pair. A good poker player does not waste chips banking two pair. Neither should a good general, when his chips are human lives. As it was, in the retreat 700 French were killed or wounded, and of the British, who were more directly in the path of the Bulgars, 1,000.

At Gevgheli the French delayed two days to allow the Serbian troops to get away and then themselves withdrew. There now no longer were any Serbian soldiers in Serbia, and the left flank of Sarrail was exposed. So both armies fell back toward Saloniki on a line between Kilindir and Boiran railroad station, and all the places we visited a week before were now occupied by the enemy. At Gravec a Bulgarian is pointing at the wicked ones who are being driven into the flames and saying, "The Allies," and at Strumnitza station in the mess hall Bulgar officers are framing John McCutcheon's sketches.

And here at Saloniki, from sunrise to sunset, the English are disembarking reinforcements and the French building barracks of stone and brick. It looks as though the retreating habit was broken.

The New York Times
January 23, 1916

A Deserted Command

An Episode on the Serbian Frontier, Where Two Boys Under Twenty with a Gun That Stuck Held Their Own

Saloniki, Greece. Dec. 10.

ON the day the retreat began from Krivolak, General Sarrail, commanding the Allies in Serbia, gave the correspondents permission to visit the French and English front. The French advanced position, and a large amount of ammunition, 600 shells to each gun, were then at Krivolak, and the English base at Doiran. We left the train at Doiran, after a luncheon en route. The Italian correspondent had been detailed as chief of commissariat. But as his idea of campaign rations was hard boiled eggs and the straw-covered flasks of his native chianti, he was removed from his command. Fortunately, after that, we were the guests of the French Army, and the horrors of war, for us, were at an end.

Our French "guide" had not informed the English a "mission militaire" was descending upon them, and in consequence at Doiran there were no conveyances to meet us. But a charming English captain commandeered for us a vast motor track. Stretched above it were ribs to support a canvas top, and by clinging to these as at home on the elevated we managed to avoid being bumped out into the road. The English captain, who seemed to have nothing else on his hands, volunteered to act as our escort and on a splendid hunter galloped ahead of and at the side of the lorry, and, much like a conductor on a sightseeing car, pointed out the objects of interest. When not explaining, he was absent-mindedly jumping his horse over swollen streams, ravines, and fallen walls. We found him much more interesting to watch than the scenery.

The scenery was desolate and bleak. It consisted of hills that opened into other hills, from the summit of which more hills stretched to a horizon entirely of mountains. They did not form ridges, but, like men in a crowd, shouldered into one another. They were of a soft rock and covered with snow, above which to the height of your waist rose scrub pine trees and bushes of holly. The rain and snow that ran down their slopes had turned the land into a sea of mud and had swamped the stone roads. In walking, for each step you took forward you skidded and slid several yards back. If you had an hour to spare you had time for a ten minutes' walk.

In our motor truck we circled Lake Dairan, and a mile from the station came to a stone obelisk. When we passed it our guide on horseback shouted to us that we had crossed the boundary from Greece and were now in Serbia. The lake is five miles wide and landlocked, and the road kept close to the water's edge. It led us through little mud villages, with houses of mud and wattle, and some of stone, with tiled roofs and rafters and beams showing through the cement. The second story projected like those of the Spanish blockhouses in Cuba and the log forts from which, in the days when there were no hyphenated Americans, our forefathers fought the Indians.

Except for some fishermen, the Serbians had abandoned these villages, and they were occupied by English army service men and infantry. The "front," which was hidden away among the jumble of hills, seemed, when we reached it, to consist entirely of artillery. All along the road the Tommies were waging a hopeless war against the mud, shoveling it off the stone road to keep the many motor trucks from skidding over a precipice, or against the cold by making shelters of it, or washing it out of their uniforms and off their persons. Shivering from ears to heels and with teeth rattling, but undaunted, they stood stripped to the waist, scrubbing their sun-tanned chests and shoulders (for they had come from the Dardanelles) with ice water. It was a spectacle that inspired confidence. When a man is so keen after water to wash in that he will kick the top off a frozen lake to get it, a little thing like a barbed-wire entanglement will not halt him.

The cold of those hills was like no cold I ever felt. Officers who had hunted in northern Russia, in the Himalayas, in Alaska, assured us that never had they so suffered. The men we passed, who were in the ambulances, were down either with pneumonia or frostbite. Many had lost toes and fingers. And it was not because they were not warmly clad. Last winter in France had taught the War Office how to dress the part; but nothing had prepared them for the cold of the Balkans. And to add to their distress, for it was all of that, there was no firewood. The hills were bare of trees, and such cold as they endured could not be fought with green twigs. It was not the brisk, invigorating cold that invites you out of doors. It had no cheery, healthful appeal to skates, toboggans and the jangling bells of a cutter. It was the damp, clammy, penetrating cold of a dungeon, of an unventilated ice chest, of a morgue. Your clothes did not warm you, the heat of your body had to warm your clothes; and warm, also, all of the surrounding hills.

Between the road and the margin of the lake were bamboo reeds as tall as lances and at the edge of these were gathered myriads of ducks. The fishermen were engaged in bombarding the ducks with rocks. They went about in a methodical fashion. All around the lake, concealed in the reeds and lifted a few feet above the water, they had raised huts on piles. These huts had a ledge or balcony in front and looked like overgrown bird houses on stilts. One fisherman waited in a boat to pick up the dead ducks, and the other hurled stones from a sling. It was the same kind of a sling as the one with which David slew Goliath. In Athens I saw small boys using it to throw stones at an electric light pole. The one the fisherman used was about eight feet long. To get the momentum he whirled it swiftly above his head as a cowboy swings a lariat and then let one end fly loose, and the stone, escaping, smashed into the mass of ducks. If it stunned or killed a duck, the human water spaniel in the boat would row out and retrieve it. To duck hunters at home the sport would chiefly recommend itself through the cheapness of the ammunition.

On the road we met relays of water carts and wagons that had been up the hills with food for the gunners at the front, and engineers were at work repairing the stone bridges or digging detours to avoid those that had disappeared. They were built to support no greater burden than a flock of sheep, an ox-cart or what a donkey can carry on his back, and the assault of the British motor-trucks and French six-inch guns had driven them deep into the mud.

After ten miles we came to what a staff officer would call an "advanced base," but which was locally designated the "Dump." At the side of the road, much of it uncovered to the snow, were stores of ammunition, "bully beef" and barbed wire. The camp bore all the signs of a temporary halting place. It was just what the Tommies called it, a dump. We had not been told then that the Allies were withdrawing, but one did not have to be a military expert to see that there was excellent reason why they should. They were so few. Whatever the force was against them, the force I saw was not strong enough to hold the ground, not that it covered, but over which it was sprinkled. There were outposts without supports, supports without reserves. A squad was expected to perform the duties of a company. Where a brigade was needed, there was less than a battalion. Against the white masses of the mountains and the desolate landscape without trees, houses, huts, without any sign of human habitation, the scattered groups of khaki only accented the bleak loneliness.

At the Dump we had exchanged for the impromptu motor truck automobiles of the French staff, and as Jimmie

Hare and I were alone in one of them, we could stop where we liked. So we halted where an English battery was going into action. It had dug itself into the side of a hill and covered itself with snow and pine branches. Somewhere on one of the neighboring hills the "spotter" was telephoning the range. The gunners could not see at what they were firing. They could see only the high hill of rock and snow at the base of which they stood shoulder high in their mud cellars. Ten yards to the rear of them was what looked like a newly made grave reverently covered with pine boughs. Through these a rat-faced young man, with the receivers of a telephone clamped to his ears, pushed his head.

"Eight degrees to the left, sir," he barked, "four thousand yards."

The men behind the guns were extemely young, but like most artillerymen, alert, sinewy, springing to their appointed tasks with swift, catlike certainty. The sight of the two strangers seemed to surprise them as much as the man in the grave had startled us. There were two boy officers in command, one certainly not yet eighteen, his superior officer still under twenty.

"I suppose you're all right," said the younger one. "You couldn't have got this far if you weren't all right."

He tried to scowl upon us, but he was not successful. He was too lonely, too honestly glad to see anyone from beyond the mountains that hemmed him in. They stretched on either side of him to vast distances, massed, barriers of white against a gray, somber sky; in front of him, to be exact, just four thousand yards in front of him, were Bulgarians he had never seen, but who were always "moving him on" and behind him lay a muddy road that led to a rail-head, that led to transports, that led to France, to the Channel and England. It was a long, long way to England. I felt like taking one of the boy officers under each arm and smuggling him safely home to his mother.

"You don't seem to have any supports," I ventured.

The child gazed around him. It was growing dark and

gloomier, and the hollows of the white hills were filled with shadows. His men were listening, so he said bravely, with a vague sweep of the hand at the encircling darkness. "Oh, they're about—somewhere. You might call this," he added with pride, "an independent command."

You well might.

"Report when ready," chanted his superior officer, aged nineteen.

He reported, and then the guns spoke, making a great flash in the twilight.

In spite of the light, Jimmie Hare was trying to make a photograph of the guns.

"Take it on the recoil," advised the child officer. "It's sure to stick. It always does stick." The men laughed, not slavishly, because the officer had made a joke, but as companions in trouble, and because when you are abandoned on a mountainside with a lame gun that jams, you must not take it lying down, but make a joke of it.

The French chauffeur was pumping his horn for us to return, and I went shamefacedly, as must the robbers who deserted the babes in the wood. In farewell I offered the boy officer the best cigars for sale in Greece, which is the worst thing one can say of any cigar. I apologized for them, but explained he must take them because they were called the "King of England."

"I would take them," said the infant, "if they were called the German Emperor."

At the door of the car we turned and waved, and the two infants waved back. I felt I had meanly deserted them, that for his life the mother of each could hold me to account.

But, as we drove away from the cellars of mud, the gun that stuck, and the "independent command," I could see in the twilight the flashes of the guns, and two lonely specks of light.

They were the King of England cigars burning bravely.

The New York Times
February 6, 1916

A Peep at the Famous St. Mihiel Salient

American Author Visiting French Trench Dug Deep in Chalk Mine Catches Glimpse of German Position, Holding of Which Has Cost Thousands of Lives

Paris, Jan. 18, 1916.

    It is an old saying that the busiest man always seems to have the most leisure. It is another way of complimenting him on his genius for organization. When you visit a real man of affairs you seldom find him surrounded by secretaries, stenographers, and a battery of telephones. As a rule, there is nothing on his desk save a photograph of his wife and a rose in a glass of water. Outside the headquarters of the general there were no gendarmes, no sentries, no panting automobiles, no mud-flecked chasseurs-a-cheval. Unchallenged, the car rolled up an empty avenue of trees and stopped beside an empty terrace of an apparently empty chateau. At one of the terraces was a pond and in it floated seven beautiful swans. They were the only living things in sight. I thought we had stumbled upon the country home of some gentleman of elegant leisure.

    When he appeared, the manner of the general assisted that impression. His courtesy was so undisturbed, his mind so tranquil, his conversation so entirely that of a polite host. You felt he was masquerading in the uniform of a general only because he knew it was becoming. He glowed with health and vigor. He had the appearance of having just come indoors after a satisfactory round on his private golf links. Instead he had been receiving reports from twenty-four different staff officers. His manner suggested he had no more serious responsibility than feeding bread crumbs to the seven stately swans. Instead he was responsible for the lives of 170,000 men and fifty miles of trenches. His duties were to feed the men three times a day with food, and all day and night with ammunition, to guard them against attacks from gases, burning oil, bullets, shells; and in counterattack to send them forward with the bayonet across hurdles of barb wire to distribute death. These were only a few of his responsibilities.

I know somewhere in the chateau there must be the conning tower from which the general directed his armies, and after luncheon asked to be allowed to visit it. It was filled with maps, in size enormous but rich in tiny details, nailed on frames, pinned to the walls, spread over vast drawing boards. But to the visitor more marvelous than the maps showing the French lines were those in which were set forth the German positions, marked with the place occupied by each unit, giving the exact situation of the German trenches, the German batteries, giving the numerals of each regiment. With these spread before him the General has only to lift the hand telephone and direct that from a spot on a map on one wall several tons of explosive shells shall drop on a spot on another map on the wall opposite. The General does not fight only at long distance from a map. Each morning he visits some part of the fifty miles of trenches. What later he sees on his map only jogs his memory. It is a sort of shorthand note. Where to you are waving lines, dots, and crosses, he beholds valleys, forests, miles of yellow trenches. A week ago, during a bombardment, a brother general advanced into the first trench. His chief of staff tugged at his cloak.

"My men like to see me here," said the general.

A shell killed him. But who can protest it was a life wasted? He made it possible for every *poilu* in a trench of 500 miles to say, "Our generals do not send us where they will not go themselves."

We left the white swans smoothing their feathers, and through rain drove to a hill covered closely with small trees. The trees were small because the soil from which they drew sustenance was only one to three feet deep. Beneath that was chalk. Through these woods was cut a runway for a toy railroad. It possessed the narrowest of narrow gauges, and its rolling stock consisted of flat cars three feet wide, drawn by splendid Percherons. The live stock, the rolling stock, the tracks and the trees on either side of the tracks were entirely covered with white clay. Even the brakesmen and the locomotive engineer who walked in advance of the horses were completely painted with it. And before we got out of the woods, so were the passengers. This railroad feeds the trenches, carrying to them water and ammunition, and to the kitchens in the rear uncooked food.

The French marquis who guided "Mon Capitaine" and myself to the trenches either had built this railroad, or owned a controlling interest in it, for he always spoke of it proudly as "my express," "my special train," "my petite vitesse." He had lately been in America buying cavalry horses. Concerning them he has a most intimate knowledge, as for years he has owned one of the famous racing stables in France. The last time I had seen him he was in silk, mounted on one of his own thoroughbreds, and the crowd, or that part of it that had backed his horse, was applauding him; and, while he waited for permission to dismount, he was smiling and laughing happily. Yesterday, when the plow horses pulled his express train off the rails, he descended and pushed it back, and, in consequence, was splashed, not by the mud of the race track but of the trenches. Nor in the misty, dripping, rain-soaked forest was there any one to applaud him. But he was still smiling and laughing, even more happily.

The trenches were dug around what had been a chalk mine, and it was difficult to tell where the mining for profit had stopped and the excavations for defense began. When you can see only chalk at your feet and chalk on either hand, and overhead the empty sky, this ignorance may be excused. In the boyaux, which began where the railroad stopped, that was our position. We walked through an endless grave with walls of clay, on top of which was a scant foot of earth. It looked like a layer of chocolate on the top of a cake.

In some places, under foot was a corduroy path of sticks, like the false bottom of a rowboat, in others we splashed through open sluices of clay and rain water. You slid and skidded and to hold yourself erect pressed with each hand against the wet walls of endless grave.

We came out upon the "Hauts de Meuse." They are called also the "Shores of Lorraine," because to that province, as are the cliffs of Dover to the County of Kent, they are a natural barrier. We were in the quarry that had been cut into the top of the heights on the side that now faces other heights held by the enemy. Behind us rose a sheer wall of chalk as high as a five-story building. The face of it had been pounded by shells. It was as undismayed as the whitewashed wall of a schoolroom at which generations of small boys have flung impertinent spit balls. At the edge of the quarry the floor was dug deeper, leaving a wall between it and the enemy, and behind this wall were the posts of observation, the nests of the machine guns, the raised step to which the men spring when repulsing an attack. Below and back of them were the shelters into which, during a bombardment, they disappear. They were roofed with great beams, on top of which were bags of cement piled three and four yards high.

Not on account of the sleet and fog, but in spite of them, the aspect of the place was grim and forbidding. You did not see, as at some of the other fronts, on the signboards that guide the men through the maze jokes and nicknames. The mess huts and sleeping caves bore no such ironic titles as the Petit Café, the Anti-Boche, Chez Maxim. They were designated only by numerals, businesslike and brief. It was no place for humor. The monuments to the dead were too much in evidence. On every front the men rise and lie down with death, but on no other front had I found them living so close to the graves of their former comrades. Where a man had fallen, there had he been buried, and on every hand you saw between the chalk huts, at the mouths of the pits or raised high in a niche, a pile of stones, a cross and a soldier's cap. Where one officer had fallen his men had built to his memory a mausoleum. It is also a shelter into which, when the shells come, they dive for safety. So that even in death he still protects them.

I was invited into a post of observation and told to make my entrance quickly. In order to exist, a post of observation must continue to look to the enemy only like part of the wall of earth that faces him. If through its apparently solid front there flashes, even for an instant, a ray of sunlight, he knows that the ray comes through a peephole, and that behind the peephole men with field glasses are watching him. And with his shells he hammers the post of observation into a shambles. Accordingly, when you enter one, it is etiquette not to keep the door open any longer than is necessary to squeeze past it. As a rule, the door is a curtain of sacking, but hands and bodies coated with clay, by brushing against it, have made it quite opaque.

The post was as small as a chart room and the light came only through the peepholes. You got a glimpse of a rack of rifles, of shadowy figures that made way for you, and of your captain speaking in a whisper. When you put your eyes to the peephole it was like looking at a photograph through a stereoscope. But, instead of seeing the lake of Geneva, the Houses of Parliament, or Niagara Falls, you looked across a rain driven valley of mud, on the opposite side of which was a hill.

Here the reader kindly will imagine three stickfuls of printed matter devoted to that hill. It was an extremely interesting hill, but my captain, who also is my censor, decides that what I wrote was entirely too interesting, especially to Germans. So the hill is "strafed." He says I can begin again vaguely with "Over there."

"Over there," said the voice in the darkness, "is St. Mihiel."

For more than a year you had read of St. Mihiel. Communiqués, maps, illustrations had made it famous and familiar. It was the town that gave a name to the German salient, to the point thrust in advance of what should be his front. You expected to see an isolated hill, a promontory, some position of such strategic value as would explain why for St. Mihiel the lives of thousands of Germans had been thrown like dice upon a board. But except for the obstinacy of the German mind, or, upon the part of the Crown Prince, the lack of it, I could find no explanation. Why the German wants to hold St. Mihiel, why he ever tried to hold it, why if it so pleases him he should not continue to hold it until his whole line is driven across the border, is difficult to understand. For him it is certainly an expensive position. It lengthens his lines of communication and increases his need of transport. It eats up men, eats up rations, eats up priceless ammunition, and it leads to nowhere, enfilades no position, threatens no one. It is like an ill-mannered boy sticking out his tongue. And as ineffective.

The physical aspect of St. Mihiel is a broad sweep of meadow land cut in half by the Meuse flooding her banks and the houses of the Ferme Mont Meuse. On each side of the salient are the French. Across the battleground of St. Mihiel I could see their trenches facing those in which we stood. For, at St. Mihiel, instead of having the line of the enemy only in front, the German has it facing him and on both flanks. Speaking not as a military strategist but merely as a partisan, if any German commander wants that kind of a position I would certainly make him a present of it.

The colonel who commanded the trenches possessed an enthusiasm that was beautiful to see. He was as proud of his chalk quarry as an admiral of his first dreadnought. He was as isolated as though cast upon a rock in mid-ocean. Behind him was the dripping forest, in front of the mud valley filled with floating fogs. At his feet in the chalk floor the shells had gouged out holes as deep as rain barrels. Other shells were liable at any moment to gouge out more holes. Three days before, when Prince Arthur of Connaught had come to tea, a shell hit outside the colonel's private cave and smashed all the tea cups. It is extremely annoying when English royalty drops in sociably to distribute medals and sip a cup of tea to have German shells invite themselves to the party. It is a way German shells have. They push in everywhere. One invited itself to my party and got within ten feet of it. When I complained, the colonel suggested absently it probably was not a German shell but a French mine that had gone off prematurely. He seemed to think being hit by a French mine rather than by a German shell made all the difference in the world. It nearly did.

At the moment the colonel was greatly interested in the fact that one of his men was not carrying a mask against gases. The colonel argued that the life of the man belonged to France, and that through laziness or indifference he had no right to risk losing it. Until this war the colonel had commanded in Africa the regiment into which criminals are drafted as a punishment. To keep them in hand requires both imagination and the direct methods of a bucko mate on a whaler. When the colonel was promoted to his present command he found the men did not place much confidence in the gas masks, so he filled a shelter with poisoned air, equipped a squad with protectors and ordered them to enter. They went without enthusiasm, but when they found they could move about with impunity the confidence of the entire command was gained.

The colonel was very vigilant against these gas attacks. He had equipped the only shelter I have seen devoted solely to the preparation of defenses against them. We learned several new facts concerning this hideous form of warfare. One was that the Germans now launch the gas most frequently at night when the men cannot see it approach, and, in consequence, before they can snap the masks into place, they are suffocated and, in great agony, die. They have learned much about the gas, but chiefly by bitter experience. Two hours after one of the attacks an officer seeking his field glasses descended into his shelter. The gas that had flooded the trenches and then floated away still lurked below. And in a moment the officer was dead. The warning was instantly flashed along the trenches from the North Sea to Switzerland, and now after a gas raid the underground shelters are attacked by counterirritants and the poison driven from ambush.

I have never seen better discipline than obtained in that chalk quarry, or better spirit. There was not a single outside element to aid discipline or to inspire morale. It had all to come from within. It had all to spring from the men themselves and from the example set by their officers. The enemy fought against them, the elements fought against them, the place itself was as cheerful as a crutch. The clay climbed from their feet to their things, was ground into their uniforms, clung to their hands and hair. The rain chilled them, the wind, cold, damp, and harsh, stabbed through their great coats. Their outlook was upon graves, their resting places dark caverns, at which even a wolf would look with suspicion. And yet they were all smiling, eager, alert. In the whole command we saw not one sullen or wistful face.

It is an old saying, "So the colonel, so the regiment."

But the splendid spirit I saw on the heights of the Meuse is true not only of that colonel and of that regiment, but of the whole 500 miles of trenches, and of all France.

The New York Times
February 13, 1916

The War That Lurks in Forest of the Vosges

Trenches and Log Barricades Set Among Moss, Fern and Sweet-Smelling Pine – Both French and German Soldiers Use Watchdogs for Sentry Duty

When speaking of their 500 miles of front, the French General Staff divide it into twelve sectors. The names of these do not appear on maps. They are family names and titles, not of certain places, but of districts with imaginary boundaries. These nicknames seem to thrive best in countries where the same race of people have lived for many centuries. With us, it is usually when we speak of mountains, as "in the Rockies," "in the Adirondacks," that under one name we merge rivers, valleys, and villages. To know the French names for the twelve official fronts may help in deciphering the communiqués. They are these:

Flanders, the first sector, stretches from the North Sea to beyond Ypres; the Artois sector surrounds Arras: the center of Picardie is Amiens; Santerre follows the valley of the Oise; Soissonais is the sector that extends from Soissons on the Aisne to the Champagne sector, which begins with Rheims and extends southwest to include Chalons; Argonne is the forest of Argonne; the Hautes de Meuse, the district around Verdun; Woevre lies between the Heights of the Meuse and the River Moselle; then come Lorraine, the Vosges, all hills and forests, and last Alsace, the territory won back from the enemy.

Of these twelve fronts, I was on ten. The remaining two I missed through leaving France to visit the French fronts in Serbia and Saloniki. According to which front you are on, the trench is of mud, clay, chalk, sandbags, or cement; it is ambushed in gardens and orchards, it winds through flooded mud flats, is hidden behind the ruins of wrecked villages, and paved and reinforced with the stones and bricks from the smashed houses.

Of all the trenches the most curious were those of the Vosges. They were the most curious because, to use the last word one associates with trenches, they are the most beautiful.

We started for the trenches of the Vosges from a certain place close to the German border. It was so close to the German border that in the inn a rifle bullet from across the border had bored a hole in the café mirror.

The car climbed steadily. The swollen rivers flowed far below us, and then disappeared, and the slopes that fell away on one side of the road and rose on the other became smothered under giant pines. Above us they reached to the clouds, below us swept grandly across great valleys. There was no sign of human habitation, not even the hut of a charcoal burner. Except for the road we might have been the first explorers of a primeval forest. We seemed as far removed from the France of cities, cultivated acres, stone bridges, and chateaux as Rip Van Winkle lost in the Catskills. The silence was the silence of the ocean.

We halted at what might have been a lumberman's camp. There were cabins of huge green logs with the moss still fresh and clinging, and smoke poured from mud chimneys. In the air was an enchanting odor of balsam and boiling coffee. It needed only a man in a Mackinaw coat with an axe to persuade us we had motored from a French village ten hundred years old into a perfectly new trading post on the Saskatchewan.

But from the lumber camp the colonel appeared, and with him in the lead we started up a hill as sheer as a church roof. The freshly cut path reached upward in short zigzag lengths. Its outer edge was shored with the trunks of the trees cut down to make way for it. They were fastened with stakes, and against rain and snow helped to hold it in place. The soil, as the path showed, was of a pink stone. It cuts easily and is the stone from which cathedrals have been built. That suggests that to an ambitious young sapling it offers little nutriment, but the pines at least seem to thrive on it. For centuries they have thrived on it. They towered over us to the height of eight stories. The ground beneath was hidden by the most exquisite moss, and moss climbed far up the tree trunks and covered the branches. They looked as though to guard them from the cold, they had been swathed in green velvet. Except for the pink path we were in a world of green—green moss, green ferns, green tree trunks, green shadows. The little light that reached from above was like that which flitters through the glass plates of an aquarium.

It was very beautiful, but was it war? We might have been in the Adirondacks, in the private camp of one of our men of millions. You expect to see the fire warden's red poster warning you to stamp out the ashes and to be careful where you throw matches. Then the path dived into a trench with pink walls, and overhead, arches of green branches rising higher and higher until they interlocked and shut out the sky. The trench led to a barrier of logs as round as a flour barrel, the openings plugged with moss and the whole hidden in fresh pine boughs. It reminded you of those open barricades used in boar hunting, and behind which the German emperor awaits the onslaught of thoroughly terrified pigs.

Like a bird nest it clung to the side of the hill, and across, a valley, looked at a sister hill a quarter of a mile away.

"On that hill," said the Colonel, "on a level with us, are the Germans."

Had he told me that among the pine-trees across the valley Santa Claus manufactured his toys and stabled his reindeer, I would have believed him. Had humpbacked dwarfs with beards peeped from behind the velvet tree trunks and doffed red nightcaps, had we discovered fairies dancing on the moss carpet, the surprised ones would have been, not we, but the fairies.

In this enchanted forest to talk of Germans and war was ridiculous. We were speaking in ordinary tones, but in the stillness of the woods our voices carried, and from just below us a dog barked.

"Do you allow the men to bring dogs into the trenches?" I asked. "Don't they give away your position?"

"That is not one of our dogs," said the Colonel. "That is a German sentry dog. He has heard us talking."

"But that dog is not across that valley," I objected.

"He's on this hill. He's not 200 yards below us."

"But, yes, certainly," said the colonel. Of the man on duty behind the log barrier he asked:

"How near are they?"

"Two hundred yards," said the soldier. The soldier grinned and, leaning over the top log, pointed directly beneath us.

It was as though we were on the roof of a house looking over the edge at some one on the front steps. I stared down through the giant pine trees towering like masts, mysterious, motionless, silent with the silence of centuries. Through the interlacing boughs I saw only shifting shadows or, where a shaft of sunlight fell upon the moss, a flash of vivid green. Unable to believe, I shook my head. Even the Boche watchdog, now thoroughly annoyed, did not convince me. As though reading my doubts, an officer beckoned, and we stepped outside the breastworks and into an intricate cat's cradle of barbed wire. It was lashed to heavy stakes and wound around the tree trunks, and, had the officer not led the way, it would have been impossible for me to get either in or out. At intervals, like clothes on a line, on the wires were strung empty tin cans, pans, and pots, and glass bottles. To attempt to cross the entanglement would have made a noise like a peddler's cart bumping over cobbles.

We came to the edge of the barb wire, and what looked like part of a tree trunk turned into a man-sized bird's nest. The sentry in the nest had his back to us and was peering intently down through the branches of the tree tops. He remained so long motionless that I thought he was not aware of our approach. But he had heard us. Only it was no part of his orders to make abrupt movements. With infinite caution, with the most considerate slowness, he turned, scowled, and waved us back. It was the care with which he made even so slight a gesture that persuaded me the Germans were as close as the colonel had said. My curiosity concerning them was satisfied. The sentry did not need to wave me back. I was already on my way.

At the post of observation I saw a dog kennel.

"There are watchdogs on our side, also," I said.

"Yes," the officer assented doubtfully. "The idea is that their hearing is better than that of the men, and in case of night attacks they will warn us. But during the day they get so excited barking at the Boche dogs that when darkness comes, and we need them, they are worn out and fast asleep."

We continued our walk through the forest and wherever we went found men at work repairing the path and pushing the barb wire and trenches nearer the enemy. In some places they worked with great caution hidden by the ferns and dragging behind them the coils of wire; sometimes they were able to work openly, and the forest resounded with the blows of axes and the crash of a falling tree. But an axe in a forest does not suggest war, and the scene was still one of peace and beauty.

For miles the men had lined the path with borders of moss of six inches wide and with strips of bark had decorated the huts and shelters. Across the tiny ravines they had thrown what in seed catalogues are called "rustic" bridges. As we walked in single file between these carefully laid borders of moss and past the shelters that suggested only a gamekeeper's lodge, we might have been on walking tour in the Alps. You expected at every turn to come upon a chalet like a Swiss clock and a patient cow and a young woman in a velvet bodice who would offer you warm milk.

Instead, from overhead, there burst suddenly the barking of shrapnel and, through an opening in the tree tops, we saw a French biplane pursued by German shells. It was late in the afternoon, but the sun was still shining and entirely out of her turn, the moon also was shining. In the blue sky she hung like silver shield, and toward her, it seemed almost to her level, rose the biplane.

She also was all silver. She shone and glistened. Like a great bird, she flung out tilting wings. The sun kissed them and turned them into flashing mirrors. Behind her the German shells burst in white puffs of smoke, feathery, delicate, as innocent-looking as the tips of ostrich plumes. The biplane ran before them and seemed to play with them as children race up the beach laughing at the pursuing waves. The biplane darted left, darted right, climbed unseen aerial trails, tobogganed down vast imaginary mountains, or, as a gull skims the crests of the waves, dived into a cloud and appeared again, her wings dripping, glistening and radiant. As she turned and winged her way back to France you felt no fear for her. She seemed beyond the power of man to harm, something supreme, superhuman. A sister to the sun and moon, the princess royal of the air.

After you have been in the trenches it seems so selfish to be feasting and drinking that you have no appetite for dinner.

But for the defenders of the forests of the Vosges you cannot feel selfish. Visits to their trenches do not take away my appetite. They increased it. The air they breathe tastes like brut champagne, and gases cannot reach them. They sleep on pillows of pine boughs. They look out only on what in nature is most beautiful. And their surgeon told me there was not a single man on the sick list. That does not mean there are no killed or wounded. For even in the enchanted forest there is no enchantment strong enough to ward off the death that approaches crawling on the velvet moss or hurtling through the tree tops.

War has no knowledge of sectors. It is just as hateful in the Vosges as in Flanders, only in Vosges it masks its hideousness with what is beautiful. In Flanders death hides in a trench of mud like an open grave. In the forest of the Vosges it lurks in a nest of moss, fern, and clean, sweet-smelling pine.

The New York Times
February 27, 1916

Blinded in Battle, But Not Made Useless

How the Soldiers of the Allies Who Must Live Forever in Darkness Are Now Taught to Become Independent

These days the streets of Paris are filled with soldiers each of whom has given to France some part of his physical self. That his country may endure, that she may continue to enjoy liberty, he has seen his arm or his leg, or both, blown off, or cut off. But when on the boulevards you meet him walking with crutches or with an empty sleeve pinned beneath his Cross of War, and he thinks your glance is one of pity, he resents it. He holds his head more stiffly erect. He seems to say, "I know how greatly you envy me!"

And who would dispute him? Long after the war is ended, so long as he lives, men and women of France will honor him, and in their eyes he will read their thanks. But there is one soldier who cannot read their thanks, who is spared the sight of their pity. He is the one who has made all but the supreme sacrifice. He is the one who is blind. He sits in perpetual darkness. You can remember certain nights that seemed to stretch to doomsday, when sleep was withheld and you tossed and lashed upon the pillow, praying for the dawn. Imagine a night of such torture dragged out over many years. With the dreadful knowledge that the dawn will never come. Imagine Paris with her bridges, palaces, parks, with the Seine, the Tuileries, the boulevards, the glittering shop windows conveyed to you only through noise. Only through the shrieks of motor horns and the shuffling of feet.

The men who have been blinded in battle have lost more than sight. They have been robbed of their independence.

They feel they are a burden. It is not only the physical loss they suffer, but the thought that no longer are they of use, that they are a care, that in the scheme of things—even in their own little circles of family and friends—there is for them no place. It is not unfair to the *poilu* to say that the officer who is blinded suffers more than the private. As a rule, he is more highly strung, more widely educated; he has seen more; his experience of the world is broader; he has more to lose. Before the war he may have been a lawyer, doctor, man of many affairs. For him it is harder than, for example, the peasant to accept a future of unending blackness spent in plaiting straw or weaving rag carpets. Under such conditions life no longer tempts him. Instead, death tempts him, and the pistol seems very near at hand.

It was to save men of the officer class from despair and suicide, to make them know that for them there still was a life of usefulness, work, and accomplishment, that there was organized in France the Committee for Men Blinded in Battle. The idea was to bring back to officers who had lost their sight, courage, hope, and a sense of independence to give them work not merely mechanical but more in keeping with their education and intelligence. The president of France is patron of the society, and on its committees in Paris and New York are many distinguished names. The French government has promised a house near Paris where the blind soldiers may be educated. When I saw them they were in temporary quarters in the Hotel de Crillon, lent to them by the proprietor. They had been gathered from hospitals in different parts of France by Miss Winifred Hold, who for years has been working for the blind in her Lighthouse in New York. She is assisted in the work in Paris by Mrs. Peter Cooper Hewitt. The officers were brought to the Crillon by French ladies, whose duty it was to guide them through the streets. Some of them also were their instructors, and in order to teach them to read and write with their fingers had themselves learned the Braille alphabet. This requires weeks of very close and patient study. And no nurse's uniform goes with it. But the reward was great.

It was evident in the alert and eager interest of the men who, perhaps, only a week before had wished to "curse God, and die." But since then hope had returned to each of them, and he had found a door open, and a new life.

And he was facing it with the same or with even a greater courage than that with which he had led his men into the battle that blinded him. Some of the officers were modeling in clay, others were learning typewriting, one with a drawing board was studying to be an architect, others were pressing their finger tips over the raised letters of the Braille alphabet. Opposite each officer, on the other side of the table, sat a woman he could not see. She might be young and beautiful, as many of them were. She might be white-haired and a great lady bearing an ancient title, from the faubourg across the bridges, but he heard only a voice.

The voice encouraged his progress, or corrected his mistakes, and a hand, detached and descending from nowhere, guided his hand, gently, as one guides the fingers of a child. The officer was again a child. In life for the second time he was beginning with A, B, and C. The officer was tall, handsome, and deeply sunburned. In his uniform of a chasseur d'Afrique he was a splendid figure. On his chest were the medals of the campaigns in Morocco and Algiers, and the crimson ribbon of the Legion of Honor. The officer placed his forefinger on a card covered with raised hieroglyphics.

"N," he announced.

"No," the voice answered him.

"M?" His tone did not carry conviction.

"You are guessing," accused the voice. The officer was greatly confused.

"No, no mademoiselle!" he protested. "Truly, I thought it was an 'M.'"

He laughed guiltily. The laugh shook you. You saw all that he could never see; inside the room the great ladies and latest American countesses, eager to help, forgetful of self, full of wonderful, womanly sympathy, and outside, the Place de la Concord, the gardens of the Tuileries, the trees of the Champs Elysees, the sun setting behind the gilded dome of the Invalides. All these were lost to him, and yet as he sat in the darkness, because he could not tell an N from an M, he laughed, and laughed happily. From where did he draw his strength and courage? Was it the instinct for life that makes a drowning man fight against an ocean? Was it his training as an officer of the Grande Armee? Was it the spirit of the French that is the one thing no German knows; and no German can ever break? Or was it the sound of a woman's voice and the touch of a woman's hand? If the reader wants to contribute something to help teach a new profession to these gentlemen, who in the fight for civilization have contributed their eyesight, write to the secretary of the committee, Mrs. Peter Cooper Hewitt, Hotel Ritz, Paris.

What is going forward at the Crillon for blind French officers is being carried on in London at St. Dunstan's, Regent's Park, for blind Tommies. At this school the classes are much larger than those in Paris, the pupils more numerous, and they live and sleep on the premises. The premises are very beautiful. They consist of seventeen acres of gardens, lawns, trees, a lake, and a stream on which you can row and swim, situated in Regent's Park and almost in the heart of London. In the days when London was further away the villa of St. Dunstan's belonged to the eccentric Marquis of Hertford, the wicked Lord Steyne of Thackeray's "Vanity Fair." It was a country estate. Now the city has closed in around it, but it is still a country estate, with ceilings by the Brothers Adam, portraits by Romney, sideboards by Sheraton, and on the lawn sheep. To keep sheep in London is as expensive as to keep racehourses, and to own a country estate in London can be afforded only by Americans. The estate next to St. Dunstan's is owned by an American lady. I used to play lawn tennis there with her husband. Had it not been for the horns of the taxicabs we might have been a hundred miles from the nearest railroad.

Instead, we were so close to Baker Street that one false step would have landed us in Mme. Tussaud's. When the war broke out the husband ceased hammering tennis balls and hammered German ships of war. He sank several—and is now waiting impatiently outside of Wilhemshaven for more.

St. Dunstan's also is owned by an American, Otto Kahn, the banker. In peace time, in the winter months, Mr. Kahn makes it possible for the people of New York to listen to good music at the Metropolitan Opera House. When war came, at his country place in London he made it next to possible for the blind to see. He gave the key of the estate to C. Arthur Pearson. He also gave him permission in altering St. Dunstan's to meet the needs of the blind to go as far as he liked.

When I first knew Arthur Pearson he and Lord Northcliffe were making rival collections of newspapers and magazines. They collected them as other people collect postal cards and cigar bands. Pearson was then, as he is now, a man of the most remarkable executive ability, of keen intelligence, of untiring nervous energy. That was ten years ago. He knew then that he was going blind. And when the darkness came he accepted the burden; not only his own, but he took upon his shoulders the burden of all the blind in England. He organized the National Institute for those who could not see. He gave them of his energy, which has not diminished; he gave them his time, his intelligence. If you ask what the time of a blind man is worth, go to St. Dunstan's and you will find out. You will see a home and school for blind men, run by a blind man. The same efficiency, knowledge of detail, intolerance of idleness, the same generous appreciation of the work of others, that he put into running *The Express* and *Standard*, he now exerts at St. Dunstan's. It has Pearson written all over it just as a mile away there is a building covered with the name of Selfridge, and a cathedral with the name of Christopher Wren. When I visited him in his room at St. Dunstan's he was standing with his back to the open fire dictating to a stenographer. He called to me cheerily, caught my hand, and showed me where I was to sit. All the time he was looking straight at me and firing questions.

"When did you leave Saloniki? How many troops have we landed? Our positions are very strong, aren't they?"

He told the stenographer she need not wait, and of an appointment he had which she was not to forget. Before she reached the door he remembered two more things she was not to forget. The telephone rang, and, still talking, he walked briskly around a sofa, avoided a table and an arm chair, and without fumbling picked up the instrument. What he heard was apparently very good news. He laughed delightedly, saying "That's fine! That's splendid!"

A secretary opened the door and tried to tell him what he had just learned, but was cut short.

"I know," said Pearson. "So-and-so has just phoned me. It's fine, isn't it?"

He took a small pad from his pocket, made a note on it, and laid the memorandum beside the stenographer's machine. Then he wound his way back to the fireplace and offered a case of cigarettes. He held them within a few inches of my hand. Since I last had seen him he had shaved his mustache and looked ten years younger, and, as he exercises every morning, very fit. He might have been an officer of the navy out of uniform. I had been in the room five minutes, and only once, when he wrote on the pad and I saw he did not look at the pad, would I have guessed that he was blind.

"What we teach them here," he said, firing the words as though from a machine gun, "is that blindness is not an 'affliction.' We won't allow that word. We teach them to be independent. Sisters and mothers spoil them! Afraid they'll bump their shins. Won't let them move about. Always leading them. That's bad, very bad. Makes them think they're helpless no good, invalids for life. We teach 'em to strike out for themselves. That's the way to put heart into them. Make them understand they're of use, that they can help themselves, help others, learn a trade, be self-supporting. We trained them to row. Some of them never had had oars in their hands except on the pond at Hempstead Heath on a bank holiday. We trained a crew that swept the river."

It was fine to see the light in his face. His enthusiasm gave you a thrill. He might have been Guy Nickells telling how the crew he coached won at New London.

"They were the best crews, too. University crews. Of course, our coxswain could see, but the crew were blind. We've not only taught them to row, we've taught them to support themselves, taught them trades. All men who come here have lost their eyesight in battle in this war, but already we have taught some of them a trade and set them up in business. And while the war lasts business will be good for them. And it must be nursed and made to grow. So we have an 'after care' committee. To care for them after they have left us. To buy raw material, to keep their work up to the mark, to dispose of it. We need money for those men. For the men who have started life again for themselves. Do you think there are people in America who would like to help those men?"

I asked, in case there were such people, to whom should they write.

"To me," he said. "St. Dunstan's, Regent's Park."

I found the seventeen acres of St. Dunstan's so arranged that no blind man could possibly lose his way. In the house, over the carpets, were stretched strips of matting. So long as a man kept his feet on matting he knew he was on the right path to the door. Outside the doors hand rails guided him to the workshops, schoolrooms, exercising grounds, and kitchen gardens. Just before he reached any of these places a brass knob on the hand rail warned him to go slow. Were he walking on the great stone terrace and his foot scraped against a board he knew he was within a yard of a flight of steps. Wherever you went you found men at work, learning a trade, or having learned one, intent in the joy of creating something, To help them there are nearly sixty ladies, who have mastered the Braille system and come daily to teach it. There are many other volunteers, who take the men on walks around Regent's Park and who talk and read to them. Everywhere was activity. Everywhere someone was helping someone; the blind teaching the blind; those who had been a week at St. Dunstan's doing the honors to those just arrived. The place spoke only of hard work, mutual help, and cheerfulness. When first you arrived you thought you had over the others a certain advantage, but when you saw the work the blind men were turning out, which they could not see and which you knew with both your eyes you never could have turned out, you felt apologetic. There were cabinets, for instance, measured in the twentieth of an inch, and men who were studying to be masseurs who, only by touch, could distinguish all the bones in the body. There was Miss Woods, a blind stenographer. I dictated a sentence to her, and as fast as I spoke she took it down on a machine in the Braille alphabet. It appeared in raised figures on a strip of paper like those that carry stock quotations. Then, reading the sentence with her fingers, she pounded it on an ordinary typewriter. Her work was faultless.

What impressed you was the number of the workers who, over their task, sang or whistled. None of them paid any attention to what the others were whistling. Each acted as though he were shut off in a world of his own. The spirits of the Tommies were unquenchable.

Brown Five was one of those privates who are worth more to a company than the Sergeant Major. He was a comedian. He looked like John Bunny, and when he laughed he shook all over, and you had to laugh with him, even though you were conscious that Brown Five had no eyes and no hands. But was he conscious of that? Apparently not. Was he disheartened? No! Some one snatched his cigarette; and with the stumps of his arms he promptly beat two innocent comrades over the head. When the lady guide interfered and admitted it was she who had robbed him, Brown Five roared in delight.

"I bashed 'em!" he cried. "Her took it, but I bashed the two of 'em!"

A private of the Munsters was wearing a net, and, as though he were quite along, singing, in a fine baritone, "Tipperary." If you want to hear real close harmony, you must listen to Southern darkies; and if you want to get the sweetness and melancholy out of an Irish chant, an Irishman must sing it. I thought I had heard "Tipperary" before several times, and that it was a march. But I found I had not heard it before, and that it is not a march, but a lament and a love song. The soldier did not know we were listening, and, while his fingers wove the meshes of the net, his voice rose in tones of the most moving sweetness. He did not know that he was facing a window, he did not know that he was staring straight out upon the City of London. But we knew and when in his rare baritone and rare brogue he whispered rather than sang the lines—

Good-bye, Piccadilly—
Farewell, Leicester Square
It's a long, long way to Tipperary

—all of his unseen audience hastily fled.

There was also Private Watts, who was mending shoes. When the week before Lord Kitchener visited St. Dunstan's, Watts had joked with him. I congratulated him on his courage.

"What was your joke?" I inquired.

"He asked me when I was a prisoner with the Germans how they fed me, and I said 'Oh, they gave me five beefsteaks a day.'"

"That was a good joke," I said. "Did Kitchener think so?"

The man had been laughing, pleased and proud. Now the blank eyes turned wistfully to my companion.

"Did his Lordship smile?" he asked.

These blind French officers and English Tommies are teaching a lesson. They are teaching men who are whining over the loss of money, health, or a job to be ashamed. It is not we who are keeping them, but they who are helping us. They are showing us how to face disaster and setting an example of real courage. Those who do not profit by it are more blind than they.

The New York Times
March 5, 1916

Verdun's Traps And Mazes

Treacherous Defenses Around the Great French Fortress, Which Germans Are Trying to Capture

Six weeks ago, when I was in Verdun, the Germans, from a distance of twenty miles, had dropped three shells into Nancy and threatened to send more. That gave Nancy a news interest which Verdun lacked. So I was intolerant of Verdun and anxious to hasten on to Nancy.

Today Nancy and her three shells are forgotten, and to all the world the place of greatest interest is Verdun. Verdun has been Roman, Austrian, and not until 1648 did she become a part of France. This is the fourth time she has been attacked by the Prussians in 1792, when she at once surrendered; again by the Germans in 1870, when after a gallant defense of three weeks, she surrendered, and in October of 1914.

She then was more menaced than attacked. It was the Crown Prince and General von Strantz with seven army corps who threatened her. General Sarrail, now commanding the allied forces in Saloniki, with three army corps and reinforced by part of an army corps from Toul, directed the defense. The attack was made upon Fort Troyon, about twenty miles south of Verdun. The fort was destroyed, but the Germans were repulsed. Four days later, Sept. 24, the real attack was made fifteen miles south of Troyon, on the village of St. Mihiel. The object of von Strantz was to break through the Verdun-Toul line, to inclose Sarrail from the south and at Revigny link arms with the Crown Prince. They then would have had the army of Sarrail surrounded.

For several days it looked as though von Strantz would succeed, but though outnumbered, Sarrail's line held, and he forced von Strantz to "dig in" at St. Mihiel. The salient of St. Mihiel still exists. It is like a dagger that failed to reach the heart but remains stuck in the flesh. On either side the French surround it. In January, from the first line of trenches to the north, I could look across the salient held by the Germans and see, on the other side of them, 800 yards away and facing us, the French trenches to the southwest.

The attack of von Strantz having failed, a week later, on Oct. 3, the Crown Prince attacked through the Forest of the Argonne between Varennes and Verdun. But this assault also was repulsed by Sarrail, who captured Varennes and with his left joined up with the Fourth Army of General Langle. The line as then formed by that victory remained much as it is today. The present attack is directed neither to the north nor south of Verdun, but straight at the forts of the city. These forts form but a part of the defenses. For twenty miles in front of Verdun have been spread trenches and barb wire. In turn, these are covered by artillery positions in the woods and on every height. Even were a fort destroyed, to occupy it the enemy must pass over a terrain every foot of which is under fire. As the defense of Verdun has been arranged, each of the forts is but a rallying point, a base. The actual fighting, the combat that will decide the struggle, will take place in the open.

Last month I was invited to one of the Verdun forts. It now lies in the very path of the drive, and to describe it would be improper. But the approaches to the fort are now what every German knows. They were more impressive even than the fort. The "glacis" of the fort stretched for a mile, and as we walked in the direction of the German trenches there was not a moment when from every side French guns could not have blown us into fragments. They were mounted on the spurs of the hills, sunk in pits, ambushed in the thick pine woods. Every step forward was made cautiously between trenches, or through mazes of barb wire and iron hurdles with bayonet-like spikes. Even walking leisurely you had to watch your step. Pits opened suddenly at your feet, and strands of barbed wire caught at your clothing. Whichever way you looked trenches flanked you. They were dug at every angle and were not further than fifty yards apart.

On one side, a half mile distant, was a hill heavily wooded. At regular intervals the trees had been cut down and uprooted and, like a woodroad, a cleared place showed. These were the nests of the "seventy-fives." They could sweep the approaches to the fort as a fire hose flushes a gutter. That a human being should be ordered to advance against such pitfalls and obstructions, and under the fire from the trenches and batteries, seemed sheer murder. Not even a cat with nine lives could survive.

The German papers tell that before this great drive upon Verdun was launched the German emperor reproduced the attack in miniature. The whereabouts and approaches to the positions they were to take were explained to the men. Their officers were rehearsed in the part each was to play. But no rehearsal would teach a man to avoid the pitfalls that surround Verdun. The open places are as treacherous as quicksands, the forests that seem to offer him shelter are a succession of traps. And if he captures one fort he but brings himself under the fire of two others.

The New York Times
November 6, 1916

President Poincaré Thanks America

While still six hundred miles from the French coast the passengers on the *Chicago* of the French line entered what was supposed to be the war zone.

In those same waters, just as though the reputation of the Bay of Biscay was not sufficiently scandalous, two ships of the line had been torpedoed. So, in preparation for what the captain tactfully called an "accident," we rehearsed abandoning ship.

It was like the fire-drills in our public schools. It seemed a most sensible precaution, and one that in times of peace, as well as of war, might with advantage be enforced on all passenger ships.

In his proclamation Commandant Mace of the *Chicago* borrowed an idea from the New York Fire Department. It was the warning Commissioner Adamson prints on theatre programmes, and which casts a gloom over patrons of the drama by instructing them to look for the nearest fire-escape.

Each passenger on the *Chicago* was assigned to a lifeboat. He was advised to find out how from any part of the ship at which he might be caught he could soonest reach it.

Women and children were to assemble on the boat deck by the boat to which they were assigned. After they had been lowered to the water, the men—who, meanwhile, were to be segregated on the deck below them—would descend by rope ladders.

Entrance to a boat was by ticket only. The tickets were six inches square and bore a number. If you lost your ticket you lost your life. Each of the more imaginative passengers insured his life by fastening the ticket to his clothes with a safety-pin.

Two days from land there was a full-dress rehearsal, and for the first time we met those with whom we were expected to put to sea in an open boat.

Apparently those in each boat were selected by lot. As one young doctor in the ambulance service put it: "The society in my boat is not at all congenial."

The only other persons originally in my boat were Red Cross nurses of the Post unit and infants. In trampling upon them to safety I foresaw no difficulty.

But at the dress rehearsal the purser added six dark and dangerous-looking Spaniards. It developed later that by profession they were bull-fighters. Any man who is not afraid of a bull is entitled to respect. But being cast adrift with six did not appeal.

One could not help wondering what would happen if we ran out of provisions and the bull-fighters grew hungry. I tore up my ticket and planned to swim.

Some of the passengers took the rehearsal to heart, and, all night, fully dressed, especially as to boots, tramped the deck. As the promenade deck is directly over the cabins, not only they did not sleep but neither did any one else.

The next day they began to see periscopes. For this they were not greatly to be blamed. The sea approach to Bordeaux is flagged with black buoys supporting iron masts that support the lights, and in the rain and fog they look very much like periscopes.

But after the passengers had been thrilled by the sight of twenty of them, they became so bored with false alarms that had a real submarine appeared they were in a mood to invite the captain on board and give him a drink.

While we still were anxiously keeping watch, a sail appeared upon the horizon. Even the strongest glasses could make nothing of it. A young, very young Frenchman ran to the bridge and called to the officers: "Gentlemen, will you please tell me what boat it is that I see?"

Had he asked the same question of an American captain while that officer was on the bridge, the captain would have turned his back. An English captain would have put him in irons.

But the French captain called down to him: "She is pilot-boat No. 28. The pilot's name is Jean Baptiste. He has a wife and four children in Bordeaux, and others in Brest and Havre. He is fifty years old and has a red nose and a wart on his chin. Is there anything else you would like to know?"

At daybreak, as the ship swept up the Gironde to Bordeaux, we had our first view of the enemy.

We had passed the vineyards and those châteaux the names of which every wine-card in every part of the world helps to keep famous and familiar, and had reached the outskirts of the city. Here the banks are close together, so close that one almost can hail those on shore; but there was a heavy rain and the mist played tricks.

When I saw a man in a black overcoat with the brass buttons wider apart across the chest than at the belt line, like those of our traffic police in summer-time, I thought it was a trick of the mist. Because the uniform that, by a nice adjustment of buttons, tries to broaden the shoulders and decrease the waist, is not being worn much in France. Not if a French sharpshooter sees it first.

But the man in the overcoat was not carrying a rifle on his shoulder. He was carrying a bag of cement, and from the hull of the barge others appeared, each with a bag upon his shoulder. There was no mistaking them. Nor their little round caps, high boots, and field uniforms of gray-green.

It was strange that the first persons we should see since we left the wharf at the foot of Fifteenth Street, North River, the first we should see in France, should not be French people but German soldiers.

Bordeaux had the good taste to burn down when the architect who designed the Place de la Concorde, in Paris, and the buildings facing it was still alive; and after his designs, or those of his pupils, Bordeaux was rebuilt. So wherever you look you see the best in what is old and the smartest in what is modern.

Certainly when to that city President Poincaré and his cabinet moved the government, they gave it a resting-place that was both dignified and charming. To walk the streets and wharfs is a continual delight. One is never bored. It is like reading a book in which there are no dull pages.

Everywhere are the splendid buildings of Louis XV, statues, parks, monuments, churches, great arches that once were the outer gates, and many miles of quays redolent, not of the sea, but of the wine to which the city gives her name.

But today to walk the streets of Bordeaux saddens as well as delights. There are so many wounded. There are so many women and children all in black. It is a relief when you learn that the wounded are from different parts of France, that they have been sent to Bordeaux to recuperate and are greatly in excess of the proportion of wounded you would find in other cities.

But the women and children in black are not convalescents. Their wounds heal slowly, or not at all.

At the wharfs a white ship with gigantic American flags painted on her sides and with an American flag at the stern was unloading horses. They were for the French artillery and cavalry, but they were so glad to be free of the ship that their future state did not distress them.

Instead, they kicked joyously, scattering the sentries, who were jet-black Turcos. As one of them would run from a plunging horse, the others laughed at him with that contagious laugh of the darky that is the same all the world over, whether he hails from Mobile or Tangiers, and he would return sheepishly, with eyes rolling, protesting the horse was a "Boche."

Officers, who looked as though in times of peace they might be gentlemen jockeys, were receiving the remounts and identifying the brands on the hoof and shoulder that had been made by their agents in America.

If the veterinary passed the horse, he was again marked, this time with regimental numbers, on the hoof with a branding-iron, and on the flanks with white paint. In ten days he will be given a set of shoes, and in a month he will be under fire.

Colonel Count René de Montjou, who has been a year in America buying remounts, and who returned on the *Chicago*, discovered that one of the horses was a "substitut," and a very bad "substitut" he was. His teeth had been filed, but the French officers saw that he was all of eighteen years old.

The young American who, in the interests of the contractor, was checking off the horses, refused to be shocked. Out of the corner of his thin lips he whispered confidentially:

"Suppose he is a ringer," he protested; "suppose he is eighteen years old, what's the use of their making a holler? What's it matter how old he is, if all they're going to do with him is to get him shot?"

That night at the station, as we waited for the express to Paris, many recruits were starting for the front. There seemed to be thousands of them, all new; new sky-blue uniforms, new soup-tureen helmets, new shoes.

They were splendidly young and vigorous looking, and to the tale that France now is forced to call out only old men and boys they gave the lie. With many of them, to say farewell, came friends and family. There was one group that was all comedy, a handsome young man under thirty, his mother and a young girl who might have been his wife or sister.

They had brought him food for the journey; chocolate, a long loaf, tins of sardines, a bottle of wine; and the fun was in trying to find any pocket, bag, or haversack not already filled. They were all laughing, the little, fat mother rather mechanically, when the whistle blew.

It was one of those shrill, long-drawn whistles without which in Europe no train can start. It had a peevish, infantile sound, like the squeak of a nursery toy. But it was as ominous as though someone had fired a siege gun.

The soldiers raced for the cars, and the one in front of me, suddenly grown grave, stooped and kissed the fat, little mother.

She was still laughing; but at his embrace and at the meaning of it, at the thought that the son, who to her was always a baby, might never again embrace her, she tore herself from him sobbing and fled—fled blindly as though to escape from her grief.

Other women, their eyes filled with sudden tears, made way, and with their fingers pressed to their lips turned to watch her.

The young soldier kissed the wife, or sister, or sweetheart, or whatever she was, sketchily on one ear and shoved her after the fleeing figure.

"Guardez mama!" he said.

It is the tragedy that will never grow less, and never grow old.

One who left Paris in October, 1914, and returned in October, 1915, finds her calm, confident; her social temperature only a little below normal.

A year ago the gray-green tidal wave of the German armies that threatened to engulf Paris had just been checked. With the thunder of their advance Paris was still shaken. The withdrawal of men to the front, and of women and children to Bordeaux and the coast, had left the city uninhabited. The streets were as deserted as the Atlantic City boardwalk in January. For miles one moved between closed shops. Along the Aisne the lines had not been dug in, and hourly from the front ambulances, carrying the wounded and French and British officers unwashed from the trenches, in mud-covered, bullet-scarred cars, raced down the echoing boulevards. In the few restaurants open, you met men who that morning had left the firing line and who, after *déjeuner* and the purchase of soap, cigarettes, and underclothes, by sunset would be back on the job. In those days Paris was inside the "fire-lines." War was in the air; you smelled it, saw it, heard it.

Today a man from Mars visiting Paris might remain here a week, and not know that this country is waging the greatest war in history. When you walk the crowded streets it is impossible to believe that within forty miles of you millions of men are facing each other in a death grip. This is so, first, because a great wall of silence has been built between Paris and the front, and, second, because the spirit of France is too alive, too resilient, occupied with too many interests, to allow any one thing, even war, to obsess it. The people of France have accepted the war as they accept the rigors of winter. They may not like the sleet and snow of winter, but they are not going to let the winter beat them. In consequence, the shop windows are again dressed in their best, the kiosks announce comedies, revues, operas; in the gardens of the Luxembourg the beds are brilliant with autumn flowers, and the old gentlemen have resumed their games of croquet, the Champs-Élysées swarms with baby-carriages, and at the aperitif hour on the sidewalks there are no empty chairs. At many of the restaurants it is impossible to obtain a table.

It is not the Paris of the days before the war. It is not "gay Paris." But it is a Paris going about her "business as usual." This spirit of the people awakens only the most sincere admiration. It shows great calmness, great courage, and a confidence that, for the enemy of France, must be disquieting. Work for the wounded and for the families of those killed in action and who have been left without support continues. Only now, after a year of bitter experience, it is no longer hysterical. It has been systematized, made more efficient. It is no longer the work of amateurs, but of those who by daily practice have become experts.

In Paris the signs of war are not nearly as much in evidence as the activities of peace. There are many soldiers; but, in Paris, you always saw soldiers. The only difference is that now they wear bandages, or advance on crutches. And, as opposed to these evidences of the great conflict going on only forty miles distant, are the flower markets around the Madeleine, the crowds of women in front of the jewels, furs, and manteaux in the Rue de la Paix.

It is not that France is indifferent to the war. But that she has faith in her armies, in her generals. She can afford to wait. She drove the enemy from Paris; she is teaching French in Alsace; in time, when Joffre is ready, she will drive the enemy across her borders. In her faith in Joffre, she opens her shops, markets, schools, theatres. It is not callousness she shows, but that courage and confidence that are the forerunners of success.

But the year of war has brought certain changes. The search-lights have disappeared. It was found that to the enemy in the air they were less of a menace than a guide. So the great shafts of light that with majesty used to sweep the skies or cut a path into the clouds have disappeared. And nearly all other lights have disappeared. Those who drive motor-cars claim the pedestrians are careless; the pedestrians protest that the drivers of motor-cars are reckless. In any case, to cross a street at night is an adventure.

Something else that has disappeared is the British soldier. A year ago he swarmed, now he is almost entirely absent. Outside of the hospital corps, a British officer in Paris is an object of interest. In their place are many Belgians, almost too many Belgians. Their new khaki uniforms are unsoiled. Unlike the French soldiers you see, few are wounded. The answer probably is that as they cannot return to their own country, they must make their home in that of their ally. And the front they defend so valiantly is not so extended that there is room for all. Meanwhile, as they wait for their turn in the trenches, they fill the boulevards and cafés.

This is not true of the French officers. The few you see are convalescents, or on leave. It is not as it was last October, when Paris was part of the war zone. Up to a few days ago, until after seven in the evening, when the work of the day was supposed to be finished, an officer was not permitted to sit idle in a café. And now when you see one you may be sure he is recovering from a wound, or is on the General Staff, and for a few hours has been released from duty.

It is very different from a year ago when every officer was fresh from the trenches—and fresh is not quite the word, either—and he would talk freely to an eager, sympathetic group of the battle of the night before. Now the wall of silence stretches around Paris. By posters it is even enforced upon you. Before the late minister of war gave up his portfolio, by placards he warned all when in public places to be careful of what they said. "Taisez-vous! Méfiez-vous. Les oreilles ennemies vous écoutent." "Be silent. Be distrustful. The ears of the enemies are listening." This warning against spies was placed in tramways, railroad-trains, cafés. A cartoonist refused to take the good advice seriously. His picture shows one of the women conductors in a street-car asking a passenger where he is going. The passenger points to the warning. "Silence," he says, "some one may be listening."

There are other changes. A year ago gold was king. To imagine any time or place when it is not is difficult. But today an American twenty-dollar bill gives you a higher rate of exchange than an American gold double-eagle. A thousand dollars in bills in Paris is worth thirty dollars more to you than a thousand dollars in gold. And to carry it does not make you think you are concealing a forty-five Colt. The decrease in value is due to the fact that you cannot take gold out of the country. That is true of every country in Europe, and of any kind of gold. At the border it is taken from you and in exchange you must accept bills. So, anyone in Paris wishing to travel had best turn over his gold to the Bank of France. He will receive not only a good rate of exchange but also an engraved certificate testifying that he has contributed to the national defense.

Another curious vagary of the war that obtains now is the sudden disappearance of the copper sou or what ranks with our penny. Why it is scarce no one seems to know. The generally accepted explanation is that the copper has flown to the trenches where millions of men are dealing in small sums. But whatever the reason, the fact remains. In the stores you receive change in postage-stamps, and, on the underground railroad, where the people have refused to accept stamps in lieu of coppers, there are incipient riots. One night at a restaurant I was given change in stamps and tried to get even with the house by unloading them as his tip on the waiter. He protested eloquently. "Letters I never write," he explained. "To write letters makes me ennui. And yet if I wrote for a hundred years I could not use all the stamps my patrons have forced upon me."

These differences the year has brought about are not lasting, and are unimportant. The change that is important, and which threatens to last a long time, is the difference in the sentiment of the French people toward Americans.

Before the war we were not unduly flattering ourselves if we said the attitude of the French toward the United States was friendly. There were reasons why they should regard us at least with tolerance. We were very good customers. From different parts of France we imported wines and silks. In Paris we spent, some of us spent, millions on jewels and clothes. In automobiles and on Cook's tours every summer Americans scattered money from Brittany to Marseilles. They were the natural prey of Parisian hotel-keepers, restaurants, milliners, and dressmakers. We were a sister republic, the two countries swapped statues of their great men—we had not forgotten Lafayette, France honored Paul Jones. A year ago, in the comic papers, between John Bull and Uncle Sam, it was not Uncle Sam who got the worst of it. Then the war came and with it, in the feeling toward ourselves, a complete change. A year ago we were almost one of the Allies, much more popular than Italians, more sympathetic than the English. Today we are regarded, not with hostility, but with amazed contempt.

This most regrettable change was first brought about by President Wilson's letter calling upon Americans to be neutral. The French could not understand it. From their point of view it was an unnecessary affront. It was as unexpected as the cut direct from a friend; as unwarranted, as gratuitous, as a slap in the face. The millions that poured in from America for the Red Cross, the services of Americans in hospitals, were accepted as the offerings of individuals, not as representing the sentiment of the American people. That sentiment, the French still insist in believing, found expression in the letter that called upon all Americans to be neutral, something which to a Frenchman is neither fish, fowl, nor good red herring.

We lost caste in other ways. We supplied France with munitions, but, as a purchasing agent for the government put it to me, we are not losing much money by it, and, until the French Government protested, and the protest was printed all over the United States, some of our manufacturers supplied articles that were worthless. Doctor Charles W. Cowan, an American who in winter lives in Paris and Nice and spends his summers in America, showed me the half section of a shoe of which he said sixty thousand pairs had been ordered, until it was found that part of each shoe was made of brown paper. Certainly part of the shoe he showed me was made of brown paper.

When an entire people, men, women, and children, are fighting for their national existence, and their individual home and life, to have such evidences of Yankee smartness foisted upon them does not make for friendship. It inspired contempt. This unpleasant sentiment was strengthened by our failure to demand satisfaction for the lives lost on the *Lusitania*, while at the same time our losses in dollars seemed to distress us so deeply. But more harmful and more unfortunate than any other word or act was the statement of President Wilson that we might be "too proud to fight." This struck the French not only as proclaiming us a cowardly nation, but as assuming superiority over the man who not only would fight, but who was fighting. And as at that moment several million Frenchmen were fighting, it was natural that they should laugh. Every nation in Europe laughed. In an Italian cartoon Uncle Sam is shown, hat in hand, offering a "note" to the German Emperor and in another shooting Haitians.

The legend reads: "He is too proud to fight the Kaiser, but not too proud to kill niggers." In London, "Too Proud to Fight" is in the music-halls the line surest of raising a laugh, and the recruiting-stations show pictures of fat men, effeminates, degenerates, and cripples labelled: "These Are Too Proud to Fight! Are You?" The change of sentiment toward us in France is shown in many ways. To retail them would not help matters. But as one hears of them from Americans who, since the war began, have been working in the hospitals, on distributing committees, in the banking-houses, and as diplomats and consuls, that our country is most unpopular is only too evident.

It is the greater pity because the real feeling of our people toward France in this war is one of enthusiastic admiration. Of all the Allies, Americans probably hold for the French the most hearty good-feeling, affection, and good-will. Through the government at Washington this feeling has been ill-expressed, if not entirely concealed. It is unfortunate. Mr. Kipling, whose manners are his own, has given as a toast: "Damn all neutrals." The French are more polite. But when this war is over we may find that in twelve months we have lost friends of many years. That over all the world we have lost them.

That does not mean that for the help Americans have given France and her Allies, the Allies are ungrateful. That the French certainly are not ungrateful I was given assurance by no less an authority than the president of the republic. His assurance was conveyed to the American people in a message of thanks. It is also a message of goodwill.

It recognizes and appreciates the sympathy shown to France in her present fight for liberty and civilization by those Americans who remember that when we fought for our liberty France was not neutral, but sent us Lafayette and Rochambeau, ships and soldiers. It is a message of thanks from President Poincaré to those Americans who found it less easy to be neutral than to be grateful.

It was my good fortune to be presented by Paul

Benazet, a close personal friend of the president, and both an officer of the army and a deputy. As a deputy before the war he helped largely in passing the bills that called for three years of military service and for heavier artillery. As an officer he won the Legion of Honor and the Cross of War. Besides being a brilliant writer, M. Benazet is also an accomplished linguist, and as President Poincaré does not express himself readily in English, and as my French is better suited to restaurants than palaces, he acted as our interpreter.

The arrival of important visitors, M. Cambon, the former ambassador to the United States, and the new prime minister, M. Briand, delayed our reception, and while we waited we were escorted through the official rooms of the Élysée. It was a half-hour of most fascinating interest, not only because the vast salons were filled with what, in art, is most beautiful, but because we were brought back to the ghosts of other days.

What we actually saw were the best of Gobelin tapestries, the best of Sèvres china, the best of mural paintings. We walked on silken carpets, bearing the fleur-de-lis. We sat on sofas of embroidery as fine as an engraving and as rich in color as a painting by Morland. The bright autumn sunshine illuminated the ormulu brass of the First Empire, gilt eagles, crowns, cupids, and the only letter of the alphabet that always suggests one name.

Those which we brought back to the rooms in which once they lived, planned, and plotted were the ghosts of Mme. de Pompadour, Louis XVI, Murat, Napoleon I, and Napoleon III. We could imagine the first emperor standing with his hands clasped behind him in front of the marble fireplace, his figure reflected in the full-length mirrors, his features in gold looking down at him from the walls and ceilings. We intruded even into the little room opening on the rose garden, where for hours he would pace the floor.

But, perhaps, what was of greatest interest was the remarkable adjustment of these surroundings, royal and imperial, to the simple and dignified needs of a republic.

France is a military nation and at war, but the evidences of militarism were entirely absent. Our own White House is not more empty of uniforms. One got the impression that he was entering the house of a private gentleman—a gentleman of great wealth and taste.

We passed at last through four rooms, in which were the secretaries of the president, and as we passed, the majordomo spoke our names, and the different gentlemen half rose and bowed. It was all so quiet, so calm, so free from telephones and typewriters, that you felt that, by mistake, you had been ushered into the library of a student or a cabinet minister.

Then in the fourth room was the president. Outside this room we were presented to M. Sainsere, the personal secretary of the president, and without further ceremony M. Benazet opened the door, and in the smallest room of all, introduced me to M. Poincaré. His portraits have rendered his features familiar, but they do not give sufficiently the impression I received of kindness, firmness, and dignity.

He returned to his desk and spoke in a low voice of peculiar charm. As though the better to have the stranger understand, he spoke slowly, selecting his words.

"I have a great admiration," he said, "for the effectiveness with which Americans have shown their sympathy with France. They have sent doctors, nurses, and volunteers to drive the ambulances to carry the wounded. I have visited the hospitals at Neuilly and other places; they are admirable.

"The one at Juilly was formerly a college, but with ingenuity they have converted it into a hospital, most complete and most valuable. The American colony in Paris has shown a friendship we greatly appreciate. Your ambassador I have met several times. Our relations are most pleasant, most sympathetic."

I asked if I might repeat what he had said. The president gave his assent, and, after a pause, as though, now that he knew he would be quoted, he wished to emphasize what he had said, continued:

"My wife, who distributes articles of comfort sent to the wounded and to families in need, tells me that Americans are among the most generous contributors. Many articles come anonymously—money, clothing, and comforts for the soldiers, and layettes for their babies. We recognize and appreciate the manner in which, while preserving a strict neutrality, your countrymen and women have shown their sympathy."

The President rose and on leaving I presented a letter from ex-President Roosevelt. It was explained that this was the second letter for him I had had from Colonel Roosevelt, but that when I was a prisoner with the Germans, I had judged it wise to swallow the first one, and that I had requested Colonel Roosevelt to write the second one on thin paper. The President smiled and passed the letter critically between his thumb and forefinger.

"This one," he said, "is quite digestible."

I carried away the impression of a kind and distinguished gentleman, who, in the midst of the greatest crisis in history, could find time to dictate a message of thanks to those he knew were neutrals only in name.

Further Reading

Applegate, Ed. *Muckrakers: A Biographical Dictionary of Writers and Editors.* Scarecrow Press, 2008.

Behrens, John C. *The Typewriter Guerrillas: Closeups of 20 Top Investigative Reports.* Nelson-Hall, 1977.

Cooper, Jr., Milton J. *Pivotal Decades: The United States, 1900 - 1920.* W. W. Norton, 1990.

Cornebise, Alfred E. *The Stars and Stripes: Doughboy Journalism in World War I.* Praeger, 1984.

Downey, Fairfax Davis. *Richard Harding Davis: His Day.* New York City: C. Scribner's Sons. 1933.

Goodwin, Doris Kearns. *The Bully Pulpit: Theodore Roosevelt, William Howard Taft, And The Golden Age of Journalism.* Simon & Schuster, 2014.

Klekowski, Ed ad Libby Klekowski. *Americans in Occupied Belgiuim, 1914-1918: Accounts of the War from Journalists, Tourists, Troops and Medical Staff.* McFarland, 2014.

Langford, Gerald. *The Richard Harding Davis Years: A Biography of A Mother and Son.* New York City: Holt, Rinehart & Winston. 1961.

Lardner, Ring and Jeff Silverman (ed.). *Lardner on War.* Lyons Press, 2003.

Link, William A. (ed.) and Susannah J. Link (ed.). *The Gilded Age and Progressive Era: A Documentary Reader.* Wiley-Blackwell, 2012.

Lubow, Arthur. *The Reporter Who Would Be King: A Biography of Richard Harding Davis.* Scribner, 1992.

Miner, Lewis S. *Mightier than the Sword: The Story of Richard Harding Davis.* Chicago, IL: A. Whitman & Co.. 1940.

Osborn, Scott Compton. *Richard Harding Davis: The Development of A Journalist.* Lexington, KY: University of Kentuicky Press. 1953.

Quinby, Henry Cole. *Richard Harding Davis: A Bibliography.* Wilmington, OH: Frazer Press, 2007.

Seal, Graham. *The Soldiers' Press: Trench Journals in the First World War.* Palgrave Macmillan, 2013.

Seelye, John D. *War Games: Richard Harding Davis and the New Imperialism.* Amherst, MA: University of Massachusetts Press. 2003.

Sullivan, Mark. *Our Times: The United States 1900 - 1925.* Scribners, 1962.

Thomas, Evan. *The War Lovers: Roosevelt, Lodge, Hearts, and the Rush to Empire, 1898.* Little, Brown 2010.

Online Collections

Chronicling America: Historic American Newspapers
http://chroniclingamerica.loc.gov/

HathiTrust Digital Library
http://www.hathitrust.org/

Internet Archive
https://archive.org/

New England Center for Investigative Reporting
http://necir.org/usa-muckraking-archive/

Project Gutenberg
http://www.gutenberg.org/

The Fund for Investigative Journalism
http://fij.org/

Unz.org
http://www.unz.org/Home/Introduction

from The Archive

Theodore Roosevelt
Wilderness, Vol. 1: Journalism 1886-1901
ISBN: 978-0-9907137-1-5 / *List Price: $24.95*
This volume is the first of two offering Roosevelt's complete and unabridged articles on the great western outdoors, which inspired one of his most important legacies: the preservation of vast swaths of America's frontier in its natural state. The collection includes writings on ranching and the cowboy life that appeared in contemporary juvenile magazines, including *Youth's Companion* and *St. Nicholas*.

Nellie Bly
Undercover: Reporting for *The New York World* **1887-1894**
ISBN: 978-0-9907137-2-2 / *List Price: $24.95*
Nellie Bly's convincing disguises gained her admission to oppressive sweatshops, underground gambling parlors, illicit adoption agencies and creepy mesmerists' parlors, all in the service of sensational headlines and the steadily rising circulation numbers boasted by the *New York World*. This fascinating collection of original, unabridged articles—compiled for the first time since their original publication--traces Bly's brief yet astounding career as an undercover journalist.

Lincoln Steffens
The System: Journalism 1897 - 1920
ISBN: 978-0-9907137-3-9 / *List Price: $24.95*
The muckraker Lincoln Steffens dug deep into business criminality and political corruption in a powerful series of articles written for *McClure's* magazine. This new collection from The Archive includes the author's detailed and dramatic pieces on the civic troubles in Chicago, Minneapolis, St. Louis, Philadelphia, Rhode Island, Wisconsin, New Jersey, Ohio, and New York.

Mark Twain
In Nevada: Journalism 1862 - 1864
ISBN: 978-0-9907137-0-8
List Price: $24.95
This new collection from The Archive reveals that even as a young and very green reporter, Twain related his surroundings and his acquaintances with uniquely wise and humorous insight, and turned the dry reporting style of a humble backwater newspaper into refined literary entertainment.

www.ingramcontent.com/pod-product-compliance
Lightning Source LLC
Chambersburg PA
CBHW021122300426
44113CB00006B/257